D0999832

‹ CANADA ›

MAJOR WORLD NATIONS
CANADA

Kevin Law

CHELSEA HOUSE PUBLISHERS
Philadelphia

Chelsea House Publishers

Contributing Author: Douglas Gordon

Copyright © 1999 by Chelsea House Publishers,
a division of Main Line Book Co.
All rights reserved.
Printed and bound in the United States of America.

3   5   7   9   8   6   4   2

Library of Congress Cataloging-in-Publication Data

Law, Kevin.
Canada / Kevin Law.
p.   cm. — (Major world nations)
Includes index.
Summary: An introduction to the geography, history, government,
economy, people, and culture of the second largest country
in the world.
ISBN 0–7910–4733–4
1. Canada—Juvenile literature.   [1. Canada.]
I. Title.   II. Series.
F1008.2.L35   1997
971—dc21   97–23556
CIP
AC

◄ C O N T E N T S ►

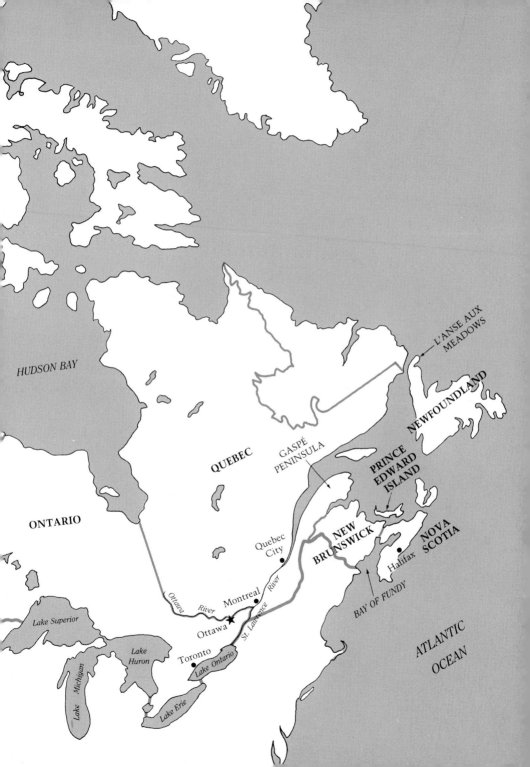

HUDSON BAY

L'ANSE AUX
MEADOWS

NEWFOUNDLAND

QUEBEC

GASPÉ
PENINSULA

PRINCE
EDWARD
ISLAND

ONTARIO

NEW
BRUNSWICK

NOVA
SCOTIA

Quebec
City

Halifax

Ottawa River

Montreal

St. Lawrence River

Ottawa

BAY OF FUNDY

Lake Superior

Lake
Huron

Toronto

Lake Ontario

ATLANTIC
OCEAN

Lake Michigan

Lake Erie

Land and People

Area   3,849,656 square miles (9,970,610 square kilometers)

Highest Point   Mount Logan, 19,850 feet (5,951 meters)

Major Rivers   St. Lawrence, Mackenzie, Fraser, Red

Capital   Ottawa

Population   30 million

Population density   7.8 persons per square mile (3 per square kilometer

Population Distribution   Urban, 77 percent; rural, 23 percent

Major Cities   Toronto, Montreal, Vancouver, Ottawa, Calgary, Quebec City, Halifax

Official Languages   English and French

National Anthem   "O Canada"

Religions   Roman Catholic, about 46 percent; Protestant, about 41 percent; others (Judaism, Islam, etc.), about 12 percent

Economy

Currency   Canadian dollar

Chief Exports   Wheat and other agricultural products, newsprint and other types of paper, lumber, petroleum, natural gas, metals, chemicals, textiles, transportation equipment, other manufactured goods.

Economic Sectors	Service sector, 72 percent of Canada's gross domestic product (GDP); industrial sector, 26 percent; agriculture, 2 percent
Per Capita Income	Approximately U.S. $20,000

Government

Form of Government	Constitutional monarchy with a parliamentary system of government; Parliament consists of 2 houses: a 104-member Senate, whose members are appointed by recommendation of the prime minister, and a 301 member House of Commons, whose members are elected by the people
Head of Government	Prime minister
Formal Head of Government	British Crown, represented by the governor-general
Cabinet	Panel of ministers appointed by the prime minister from the majority party in Parliament
Voting Rights	All Canadian citizens over age 18 can vote

◄HISTORY AT A GLANCE►

8000 B.C.	The Ice Age ends; Paleo-Indian cultures develop.
circa A.D. 1000	Vikings establish a settlement at L'Anse aux Meadows in Newfoundland.
1497	John Cabot reaches Canada's Atlantic coast.
1534	Jacques Cartier sails into the Gulf of St. Lawrence.
1605	French settlers establish Port Royal in Nova Scotia.
1608	Samuel Champlain establishes the settlement of Quebec on the St. Lawrence River.
1763	The Treaty of Paris forces France to surrender most of New France to Great Britain.
1775	The American Revolution begins; an American invasion of Canada fails.
1791	The Constitutional Act divides Quebec into Upper Canada and Lower Canada.
1793	Alexander Mackenzie crosses Canada to the Pacific coast.
1812	Lord Selkirk establishes a large settlement at Red River in Manitoba.
1812–15	The War of 1812 is fought between the United States and Great Britain; U.S. attempts to occupy Canada fail.

1837   Rebellions in Upper Canada and Lower Canada are repressed.

1840   The Act of Union unites Upper Canada and Lower Canada into the Province of Canada.

1848   The provinces of Canada and Nova Scotia achieve responsible government.

1848   Gold is discovered in the Fraser River valley.

1867   The British North American Act (Confederation) establishes the Dominion of Canada.

1869   The Dominion of Canada purchases western lands from the Hudson's Bay Company.

1870   Louis Riel leads the Red River uprising.

1870   The Province of Manitoba is added to the Dominion.

1871   The Province of British Columbia is added to the Dominion.

1873   The Province of Prince Edward Island is added to the Dominion.

1885   Canada's transcontinental railway is completed.

1885   Louis Riel leads the unsuccessful Saskatchewan Rebellion.

1897   The discovery of gold in the Klondike spurs the Yukon gold rush.

1905   The provinces of Saskatchewan and Alberta are added to the Dominion.

1914–18   More than 600,000 Canadians serve in the Allied forces during World War I; more than 60,000 die.

1929   The Great Depression begins.

1931	The Statute of Westminster gives Canada complete independence from Great Britain.
1939–45	More than 1 million Canadians serve in World War II; almost 100,000 die.
1945	Canada becomes a founding member of the United Nations.
1949	Canada, the United States, and 10 western European nations form the North American Treaty Organization (NATO).
1950–53	Canadian troops serve in the UN force during the Korean War.
1965	Canada adopts a new national flag.
1982	The Constitution Act is passed.
1988	The 1988 Winter Olympics are held in Calgary, Alberta.
1992	Voters in the Northwest Territories approve the establishment of Nunavut, a self-governing homeland for the Inuit.
1993	A. Kim Campbell becomes Canada's first female prime minister, but loses office in the national elections the same year. In those same elections, two regional parties (the Bloc Quebecois, a Quebec separatist party, and the Reform Party of western conservatives) become the leading opposition groups in the House of Commons.
1994	The North American Free Trade Agreement (NAFTA) takes effect.
1997	Following the national election, the Liberal Party returns to power but with only a slight majority. The Reform Party replaces the Bloc Quebecois as the official opposition.

Much of the Canadian wilderness remains unspoiled, providing spectacular scenery for visitors from the nation's thriving cities and productive farmlands.

Canada and the World

Canada covers more land area than any other nation except Russia. It sweeps from the Atlantic Ocean on the east to the Pacific Ocean on the west and from its border with the United States on the south to the huge arctic wilderness in the north.

It is a land of great variety. In the east, sandy beaches and rocky coves dot the coastline. Vast forests of pine, fir, spruce, and other trees cover the low mountains of northern Quebec. Canada's largest cities and major industrial centers are found along the Great Lakes and upper St. Lawrence River in the southern parts of Ontario and Quebec. The prairies of central Canada extend about 800 miles (1,280 kilometers) across Alberta and Saskatchewan to the foothills of the Rocky Mountains. On these prairies, known as "Canada's breadbasket," farmers grow wheat and other grains. In the west, towering mountains, lush forests, and wild rivers create a region of great natural beauty.

Canada's copious natural resources are responsible for its economic wealth. Forests support a thriving lumber and paper industry. The rich soil in the prairie region makes Canada one of the world's leading wheat producers. Valuable stores of petroleum, zinc ore, and other minerals provide raw materials for Canada's important industries as well as income from export to other nations. And Canada's

With teams in Toronto and Montreal, Major League Baseball has become popular in Canada. This is just one example of the strong U.S. cultural influence — a fact that worries many Canadians.

rivers are an excellent source of hydroelectric power, which does not pollute the environment.

For its enormous area, however, Canada has relatively few people — only 30 million. About 80 percent of these people live within 310 miles (500 kilometers) of the southern border. The harsh terrain and severe climate in much of the northern part of the nation discourage many people from living there.

Like its landscape, Canada's population is varied. The 2 largest groups are Canadians of British descent, who make up about 40 percent of the population, and Canadians of French descent, who account for about 27 percent. The first French and British colonists reached the Atlantic coast of Canada in the 16th century. There they encountered Indians and, much later, the Inuit, or Eskimos, the native peoples of northern Canada. Indians and Inuit account for only about two percent of the population today. Many other ethnic groups — in fact, almost every known group — are represented among Canada's people. The Canadian government has always encouraged immigration, and through the centuries people from all over the world have accepted the invitation.

The name *Canada* probably comes from the Iroquois Indian word *kanata*, which means community. Ironically, one of Canada's greatest challenges as a nation has been to develop a sense of community, of unity, among all of its regions and people. For example, people in the eastern and western provinces have often felt ignored by the central federal government.

In addition, Canada remained a collection of separate colonies and provinces until the Dominion of Canada was established by a union, or confederation, of the provinces in 1867. Although the United States declared itself independent of Great Britain in 1776, the process of separation from the mother country proceeded much more gradually in Canada. The provinces of Canada never joined together to fight as one for independence.

But the most serious challenge to national unity continues to come, as it has for centuries, from the province of Quebec. Quebec is the center of French-speaking culture in Canada. Frustrated by what they feel is unjust domination by English-speaking Canada, many Quebecois (residents of Quebec) support a movement that seeks to establish Quebec as a separate nation independent from the rest of Canada. Much of their dissatisfaction can be traced back to the early days of Canadian history, when French and British explorers and settlers vied for control over the new land. Even when France gave up all claims to Canadian colonies in the Treaty of Paris in 1763, French speakers tenaciously held on to their culture and language. They continue to do so to this day.

Another challenge to Canada's national identity and unity comes from its relationship with the United States. Since the 1800s this relationship has been marked by friendship and cooperation. The Canada-U.S. border is the world's longest unguarded boundary between two nations. The United States is Canada's most important trading partner, and the two nations cooperate in matters of national defense.

Today, however, many Canadians are concerned with what they see as U.S. domination of Canada's culture and economy. They feel that Canadians need to work harder to maintain control of their own economy and to preserve their unique cultural identity.

A majestic full moon rises over the city of Toronto on the shores of Lake Ontario. On the left, the tallest man-made structure in the world, the CN Tower, affords visitors a spectacular view of Canada's largest and fastest-growing city.

The Canadian Landscape

Canada's 3,849,656 square miles (9,970,610 square kilometers) are bounded on the east by the Atlantic Ocean, on the west by Alaska and the Pacific Ocean, on the north by the Arctic Ocean, and on the south by the continental United States. From the Atlantic to the Pacific, Canada stretches some 3,223 miles (5,189 kilometers), from Cape Spear in Newfoundland to Mount St. Elias in the Yukon, near the Alaskan border. Canada is believed to have the longest total ocean coastline of any country in the world. More than 36,000 miles (57,960 kilometers) of shoreline on the mainland and another 115,133 miles (185,364 kilometers) of coastline on its islands, including the arctic islands, which extend from Greenland to the Alaskan border, ensure Canada's access to the sea.

Canada also has more lakes than the rest of the world combined. The three largest lakes on Canadian territory are Great Bear Lake, Great Slave Lake, and Lake Winnipeg. Many lakes in the more remote reaches have not yet been named. Canada also has some of the world's highest and most rugged mountains, sweeping prairies, dense woodlands, rocky coastlines, sandy beaches, and an enormous arctic wilderness.

The Province of Quebec was among the first areas settled in Canada, and the region remains dotted with small family farms and the churches of its original French Catholic settlers. In the background rises the Rock of Percé, just offshore in the Atlantic Ocean.

Canada is divided politically into 10 provinces and 2 territories. Moving from east to west, the provinces are Newfoundland, Nova Scotia, Prince Edward Island, New Brunswick, Quebec, Ontario, Manitoba, Saskatchewan, Alberta, and British Columbia. The two territories—the Yukon Territory in the far west and the Northwest Territories—cover northern Canada.

Such a huge country contains a wide variety of topography (natural land features). Besides the political division into provinces and territories, Canada can also be divided into six distinct topographical regions: the Atlantic Provinces, the St. Lawrence and southern Ontario lowlands, the Canadian Shield, the arctic north, the central plains, and the western cordillera.

The Atlantic Provinces

The Atlantic Provinces—Newfoundland, Prince Edward Island, Nova Scotia, and New Brunswick—lie on the Atlantic Ocean. They are Canada's easternmost and smallest provinces. Prince Edward Island, Nova Scotia, and New Brunswick are sometimes called the Maritime Provinces. They were the first part of Canada to be settled by Europeans.

They are a rugged area of low, forested mountains, which are a continuation of the Appalachian Mountains of the eastern United States, and some fertile valleys. The mountains here are old, in geologic terms, meaning that they were formed long ago—some 280 million years ago, in fact—and have been worn down over the ages. They range in height from 500 feet (150 meters) to 4,160 feet (1,270 meters).

Only Prince Edward Island has any large areas of flat farmland, making farming an important economic activity on the island. Prince Edward Island is known for its potatoes, dairy products, and beef. In western Nova Scotia, the Annapolis lowlands support apple orchards and dairy farms. The land in New Brunswick is thin, rocky, and generally not very fertile, but sections of the St. John River valley produce potatoes, dairy products, beef, poultry, hogs, and vegetables.

The St. Lawrence and Southern Ontario Lowlands

Canada's most populous region, the area around the St. Lawrence River and the Great Lakes, covers only 1.3 percent of the total area of the nation. The flat-to-rolling countryside holds Canada's only large forests of deciduous trees (trees that shed their leaves at the end of the growing cycle). Varieties include maple, oak, beech, hickory, and walnut. Deer and small woodland animals live in these forests.

The region also has some excellent farmlands, where fertile soil and a relatively mild climate allow farmers to produce high yields of corn, oats, barley, tobacco, and a wide variety of fruits and vegetables. Dairy farms are also important.

The St. Lawrence River and Great Lakes form one of the world's major inland waterways. Oceangoing ships sail from the Atlantic Ocean all the way to the Great Lakes, transporting huge quantities of grain, iron ore, coal, and other goods and raw materials. These

Two tractors harvest wheat in Saskatchewan, one of the fertile Prairie Provinces. The area is part of the interior plains region of North America, which includes the Great Plains in the United States.

deep lakes were formed around the end of the last ice age, approximately 10,000 years ago. During the ice ages, vast sheets of ice (glaciers) covered North America, weighing down the land and scraping its surface away. When the ice retreated, the sea rushed inland to carve out the great waterway. Today, the Great Lakes (Ontario, Erie, Huron, Michigan, and Superior) are the largest areas of fresh water in the world. Canada and the United States share the lakes.

The Canadian Shield

The Canadian Shield is the huge horseshoe-shaped basin that curves around Hudson Bay from the arctic to the coast of Newfoundland. This region, which covers about half of Canada, is a land of rolling hills, crystal-clear lakes, vast marshes, and rushing rivers. Its geography was also created by the retreat of glaciers at the end of the last ice age. The soil is generally poor in nutrients and full of rocks, making it ill suited for farming. Evergreen forests cover much of the land, providing a home for moose, deer, elk, and many other wild animals.

The Canadian Shield has been called Canada's mineral storehouse because its rocks hold much of the nation's mineral wealth, including iron ore, nickel, copper, platinum, cobalt, gold, silver, uranium, and zinc.

The Arctic North

Canada's northernmost region is mostly *tundra*. No full-size trees grow on the tundra, for a few feet below the surface is a layer of permanently frozen subsoil called permafrost. Above this rock-hard layer, a thin covering of soil supports only mosses, lichens, and hardy shrubs that burst forth in a brief summer growing season when the surface thaws and turns to a coating of mucky black soil. During the summer, many varieties of birds nest on the tundra. In the winter, however, most migrate south, except for hardy species such as snowy owls and ptarmigans, whose white winter feathers help them blend into the surrounding snow. Several distinctive animal species make their homes on the tundra, including musk oxen, caribou, arctic wolves, polar bears, and sea mammals such as seals and walruses. Most of Canada's Inuit also live here.

For thousands of years there were tribes of Inuit whose way of life depended on the huge herds of caribou that migrated across the tundra each year on their way to and from their feeding grounds. These herds were an impressive spectacle. Caribou may be five feet high from shoulder to hoof, and both male and female caribou bear an enormous set of antlers, which adds to their imposing appearance. The Inuit of the Northwest Territories lived on caribou meat. They also fashioned fishhooks from the antlers and knives from the bones, used the tendons for thread, and made boots from the hides. The caribou, in turn, fed on the mosses and lichens that blanketed the tundra during the summer, scraping snow away from the buried moss in the winter. This fragile balance of life between people, land, and animals first broke down when the Inuit obtained rifles with which they slaughtered the caribou in great numbers. The environment has been further threatened in recent years by increasing oil and gas exploration in the arctic north, which causes pollution and reduces the available habitat. In addition, buried pipelines warm the ground and break down the permafrost.

The Central Plains

West of the Canadian Shield lie the central plains. These wide grasslands, or *prairies* (the French word for meadows), spread across southern Manitoba, Saskatchewan, and Alberta. For this reason, these provinces are sometimes called the Prairie Provinces.

Farmers have plowed most of the prairie and now grow wheat and other grains in its rich black soil. In other areas, cattle graze on undisturbed grasslands. The central plains region also holds important mineral resources, mainly petroleum, natural gas, and coal.

The Western Cordillera

West of the central plains, the peaks of the western *cordillera* (the Spanish word for mountain range) rise majestically to the sky. The highest mountains in this region are those of the Rocky Mountain range, part of a chain extending from northern Alaska to New Mexico. In Canada, the Rockies range from about 7,000 feet (2,100 meters) to more than 12,000 feet (3,660 meters) above sea level. Mount

Robson in eastern British Columbia is the tallest of the Canadian Rockies, reaching a height of 12,972 feet (3,954 meters) above sea level.

The western cordillera region also includes the Coast Mountains in British Columbia and the St. Elias Mountains in the Yukon. The St. Elias range boasts Canada's highest peak, Mount Logan, which towers 19,524 feet (5,951 meters) above sea level. Glaciers cover much of the St. Elias Mountains.

Along the coast of British Columbia, numerous natural inlets called fjords provide access by sea to Canada's most majestic and most commercially valuable forests. Important tree species include red cedar, hemlock, and other evergreens.

Climate

Canada's climate is as varied as its topography. In most of the country, winter is the longest season. The more northerly the area, the longer and colder the winters and the shorter the summers. Interestingly, the Prairie Provinces receive the most snow; although it is

Winters are long in Canada, and snow covers the ground for nearly half the year in many areas. Although the average winter temperatures are lowest in the Arctic region, very little snow falls there.

farther north and has lower temperatures, the arctic region gets very little precipitation of any kind. In the coastal regions, the oceans help moderate the climate, making winters warmer and summers cooler than in the interior.

Each topographical region has its own particular weather patterns. The Atlantic Provinces receive steady precipitation year-round, and ocean breezes keep the temperature fairly low in summer. In southern Ontario and Quebec, the climate is generally humid, with hot summers and cold winters. There, temperatures in January average about 14°F (−10°C), and during the summer the average temperature is near 68°F (20°C). The Prairie Provinces usually experience short, warm summers, with temperatures from 65° to 68°F (18° to 20°C) and long, cold winters, with temperatures of −5° to 5°F (−20° to −15°C). On the Pacific Coast, summers are cool and fairly dry; winters are usually mild, cloudy, and wet.

In the west, moisture-laden winds from the Pacific Ocean meet the steep Rocky Mountain range and rise, dropping as much as 195 inches (500 centimeters) of rain in certain places. Generally there is more rain than snow in this region, and the average is 60 to 100 inches (152 to 254 centimeters). Except for the western Pacific region, most precipitation in Canada is in the form of snow, which covers the areas east of the Rockies for three to six months of the year. In the arctic and subarctic regions, winters are very long and cold, as temperatures drop far below freezing and summer temperatures seldom climb above 50°F (10°C). Although there is almost never more than two inches (five centimeters) of precipitation per month in the arctic regions, the area is cloaked with snow for more than half the year.

Cities

About 60 years ago, half of Canada's people lived in rural areas, on farms or in small communities. But today, three-fourths of Canadians live in urban areas. Over 32 percent of them live in Canada's

One of the most striking of Toronto's modern buildings is its City Hall, built in 1965 and designed by noted Finnish architect Viljo Revell.

3 largest cities—Toronto, Montreal, and Vancouver. This shift occurred mainly because manufacturing industries have rapidly grown in the cities since the 1940s, attracting workers from the countryside. Canada now has 44 urban areas with more than 100,000 people.

Canada's largest city, Toronto, lies on the shores of Lake Ontario in the Province of Ontario. Founded in 1792, the city was originally known as York, and its location in a natural harbor on Lake Ontario made it a major center of trade and transportation from the beginning. As Canada grew, so did Toronto's importance. It is now the nation's center of industry and finance. Major industries include printing and publishing; manufacturing automobiles and trucks, machinery, electrical equipment, rubber and plastic products, furniture and other wood products, and clothing; fabricating metals; and processing food and beverages. The Canadian Stock Exchange, one of the world's busiest, is located in Toronto.

As an old city, Toronto has a mix of the modern and the antique. Interesting modern structures include the CN (Canadian National) Tower, the tallest freestanding building in the world at 1,816 feet

(553 meters); City Hall; the Ontario Science Centre; and Roy Thomson Hall. Toronto is also one of Canada's major cultural centers, boasting the University of Toronto, the Toronto Symphony Orchestra, the National Ballet of Canada, the Canadian Opera Company, the Royal Ontario Museum, and the Art Gallery of Ontario.

Montreal, Canada's second-largest city, is a little more than 300 miles (480 kilometers) northeast of Toronto. Located on an island at the convergence of the St. Lawrence and the Ottawa rivers, Montreal was once the world's largest inland seaport. Today, it is still a major center of industry, commerce, finance, transportation, and the arts.

Founded in 1642 by Jesuit missionaries, the city rapidly became the center of the fur trade and the major embarkation point for the French *voyageurs* (voyagers) on their trading expeditions to the west, north, and south. At the time of Montreal's founding and for almost two centuries thereafter, heavy rapids in the St. Lawrence River made it impossible for ships to travel any farther upriver. The construction of the Lachine Canal opened the St. Lawrence and the Great Lakes to oceangoing vessels and set the stage for Montreal's development into a world-class city. Montreal is now Canada's second-busiest port and an industrial center. Major industries include food and beverages, clothing, electronics, transportation equipment, and chemicals.

As the second-largest French-speaking city in the world (Paris is the largest), Montreal is also one of the hubs of French-Canadian culture. Some visitors claim the city resembles cities in Europe. About two-thirds of the city's population is of French descent. Major French-language newspapers, two French-Canadian universities, and the Quebec National Library are based in Montreal. Montreal is also home to the leading French-Canadian theater organization, Le Théâtre du Nouveau Monde; the Montreal Symphony Orchestra; and Les Grands Ballets Canadiens.

Many of Montreal's oldest buildings were demolished in the 1960s as part of an extensive urban modernization program. In their place were erected skyscrapers and modern buildings, such as the Place de Ville Marie, a shopping, office, and entertainment complex.

Many old homes and neighborhoods remain, however, lending Montreal an Old World charm. Near the port, the city's Old Town section has been restored and is now a lively center of nightlife. In 1967, Montreal hosted Expo 67, a world's fair held to mark Canada's centennial celebration. The 1976 Summer Olympics were also held in Montreal.

More than 3,000 miles (4,800 kilometers) west of Montreal, Vancouver, Canada's third-largest city, is located on a peninsula where the Fraser River empties into the Pacific Ocean. Its deep, sheltered natural harbor has made it Canada's busiest seaport and the industrial, commercial, and financial center of the west coast province of British Columbia. The port handles the bulk of Canada's exports to nations in the Pacific Ocean, particularly Japan. Important industries include wood, paper, furniture, food and beverages, machinery, and transportation equipment.

Compared to Toronto and Montreal, Vancouver is a relatively young city. It was founded in 1885 as the western terminus of the Canadian Pacific transcontinental railway. Because of the railroad, the city grew rapidly. By the 1920s it was already the third-largest city in Canada.

Vancouver has 138 public parks, the most famous of which is scenic Stanley Park. These parks, combined with the city's location on the ocean and near the Coast Mountains, offer its residents many opportunities for outdoor recreation. Vancouver also has much to offer in the way of culture, with two universities, a symphony orchestra, an opera association, and museums and art galleries. In 1986, the city hosted Expo 86, a fair that drew millions of tourists from all over the world.

The capital of Canada and the second-largest city in Ontario, Ottawa (along with Hull, just across the Ottawa River in Quebec) is also Canada's fourth-largest urban area. Located 100 miles (160 kilometers) southwest of Montreal, Ottawa was known as Bytown when England's queen Victoria declared it the capital of the British province of Canada. When the Dominion was formed in 1867, Canadians renamed the city Ottawa and chose it to be the national capital.

Ottawa's major economic activities are government service and tourism. Tourists can visit the parliament buildings, the National Arts Centre, and the National Gallery, or they can simply enjoy the beauty of the city's many parks.

Also on a river, 225 miles (360 kilometers) northeast of Ottawa, lies the capital of Quebec Province, Quebec City. Canada's oldest city and a hub of French-Canadian culture and tradition, it is located on the northern bank of the St. Lawrence River on a massive bluff known as Cape Diamond, which rises some 300 feet (91 meters) above the river. The city's founder, Samuel de Champlain, chose this spot because it was easy to defend.

The first settlement, established in 1608, consisted of a trading post and several houses, surrounded by fortifications. It quickly became the center of the Canadian fur trade and of the colony of New France. In 1659, Bishop Laval established the Roman Catholic church of New France in Quebec City. The church had a tremendous influence on the development of the city and of the entire province and remains a major force today.

Quebec City was the site of the decisive battle that ended the struggle between France and Great Britain over control of Canada. In 1759, during the Seven Years' War, a British force commanded by General James Wolfe scaled the heights of Cape Diamond and engaged the French defenders on the Plains of Abraham, which despite its biblical-sounding name was merely a field owned by a man named Abraham Martin. The British decisively defeated the French

The Old World charm of Quebec City's narrow streets and carefully preserved buildings attracts both tourists and city residents looking for a relaxing stroll.

in a brief, bloody rout, beginning the era of British rule over all of Canada. This defeat not only doomed France's hopes for a prosperous colony in the New World, it also laid the groundwork for alienating French Canadians from the British government of their colony. Although the British allowed the inhabitants of the city to keep their language, religion, and French system of law, the effects of that long-ago military defeat persist to this day, as demonstrated by the Quebecois separatist movement, which is based in Quebec City.

Today, Quebec City is divided into two main areas—the Old City and modern Quebec City. The Old City is surrounded by restored fortifications that make Quebec City the only walled city in North America. It consists of two sections. The Lower Town, lying at the foot and on the slopes of Cape Diamond, is the old commercial and residential center. Many historic buildings in the Lower Town have been restored, and the area is a popular spot for shopping, dining, and just strolling. The Upper Town, at the top of Cape Diamond, is another preserved area of narrow cobblestone streets and old buildings. Here sits the Citadelle, a star-shaped fortress that overlooks the city and the Plains of Abraham, now a popular park. Here also is Quebec City's most recognizable landmark—the stately Château Frontenac, a huge hotel built in 1892 on the site of Samuel de Champlain's former residence. An outdoor elevator, the *funiculaire*, connects the Lower Town and Upper Town.

Beyond the city walls lies modern Quebec City, with all the trappings of a major Canadian city. Here are a convention center, an underground shopping gallery, several luxurious high-rise hotels, and the National Assembly, Quebec's provincial legislature.

In the winter of 1988, television introduced millions of people throughout the world to the less familiar Canadian city of Calgary, 400 miles (640 kilometers) east of Vancouver. For Calgary was the host of the 1988 Winter Olympics, and during the games satellites beamed images of this beautiful city to every corner of the globe. For some people, however, the Olympic coverage was not their first exposure to Calgary. The Calgary Stampede, the world's most famous rodeo, focuses attention on the city every year.

Located in the foothills of the Canadian Rockies, at the western edge of Canada's prairies, the city of over 750,000 is the center of Canada's petroleum industry. Hundreds of Canadian oil and gas companies have offices here. The petroleum industry accounts for much of Calgary's modern steel-and-glass downtown area. During the western oil boom of the 1970s, many residents were worried that the corresponding building boom would threaten Calgary's traditions and history. But the city government made efforts to preserve important examples of pioneer architecture, and today the new and old coexist in harmony.

Planners have also preserved much open space within the city. For instance, the Stephen Avenue pedestrian mall is a six-block area of open space, trees, benches, small shops, and restaurants in the heart of the downtown area. Prince's Island, a park with trees and

<33>

The Calgary Stampede, one of the world's best-known rodeos, preserves the city's rugged frontier past and attracts entrants from around the globe.

streams, is located only three blocks from downtown and is a favorite lunchtime spot of Calgary's office workers.

Calgary was founded in 1875 by the Northwest Mounted Police (now known as the Royal Canadian Mounted Police), who were sent to deal with whiskey traders who were creating trouble with the Plains Indian tribes and to pave the way for thousands of eastern Canadians who wanted to homestead in the west. They built a fort, which they named after Calgary Bay in Scotland.

Calgary was no more than a minor settlement until the transcontinental railroad connected it to the rest of Canada in 1883. It then began to grow rapidly, when many people who had planned on passing through decided to stay. In 1914, the first major oil discovery in the Turner Valley just south of Calgary spurred its development into a true city. Since then, the petroleum industry has continued to fuel Calgary's growth.

Far to the east, the growth of Halifax, the capital of Nova Scotia and the largest city in the Atlantic Provinces, was assured by the presence of another sort of natural resource—one of the world's largest and best deep-water harbors, which made it an important shipping port for eastern Canada. From its earliest days as an Indian fishing camp known as Chebucto, or "at the biggest harbor," to World War II, when it was a major British naval base, Halifax has been tied to the sea.

Halifax was founded in 1749 by British colonel Edward Cornwallis, who led a group of about 3,000 British settlers in 20 ships. At the time of Cornwallis's arrival, Nova Scotia was dominated by French settlers, who were protected by a French garrison at Louisbourg, on the eastern part of the peninsula. By the time British control of Canada was firmly established in 1763, most French settlers had been driven from Nova Scotia. Halifax quickly became the commercial, administrative, and military center of Canada's Atlantic coast.

The British military presence, combined with a thriving civilian shipbuilding industry, helped Halifax grow steadily throughout the 18th and 19th centuries. When World War I broke out in 1914, the city became a vital link in the supply line between North America and the Allied nations of Europe. During this period Halifax suffered its worst disaster. In December 1917, the supply ship *Mont Blanc*, loaded with 2,500 tons of explosives, collided with a Belgian ship, the *Imo*, in Halifax harbor. The resulting explosion, felt more than

50 miles away, leveled the northern part of the city and left 2,000 dead, 9,000 injured, and more than 6,000 homeless. This tragedy, known today simply as "the Explosion," was the largest man-made explosion of any kind until the detonation of the first atomic bomb over Hiroshima in 1945. Today, Haligonians (residents of Halifax) commemorate the Explosion annually.

After the Explosion, Halifax was quickly reconstructed and resumed its importance as the center of Canada's maritime industry. In World War II, the harbor again served as the main preparation area for Allied supply convoys to Europe.

Halifax remains an important military and commercial port. It has grown considerably over the past several decades and now has a population of more than 330,000. Despite the construction of many modern high-rise buildings and sprawling shopping centers, it remains a small city where people can enjoy all the advantages of city life without the disadvantages that come with overcrowding and excessively rapid growth. Haligonians have made a special effort to preserve and restore their historical landmarks. They even passed an ordinance in 1973 prohibiting the building of structures that would obscure certain views. Of particular historical interest is the old waterfront area, which contains shops, restaurants, museums, and dock sites for restored sailing vessels.

Jacques Cartier of France landed on the Gaspé Peninsula in 1534. He promptly claimed the land for France and introduced Christianity to the native Indian population.

Natives, Explorers, and Settlers

Canada's history is a long and colorful tale filled with exciting stories that describe how a vast wilderness developed into one of the world's great nations. The first people to live in Canada were prehistoric wanderers. Scientists called archaeologists, who study the remains of past civilizations, think that these first people came to Canada from eastern Asia.

The migration began 30,000 to 40,000 years ago, when the continents of Asia and North America were connected by a land bridge. First animals crossed the land bridge, followed by the people who hunted them. Gradually, these people moved south into the plains and forests of Canada and the rest of North America. By the end of the last ice age, about 8,000 B.C., the massive ice glaciers that once covered most of Canada had melted, raising the level of the oceans and flooding the land bridge.

The earliest-known descendants of the prehistoric wanderers are called Paleo-Indians. They lived in small tribes and hunted large animals, such as bison and caribou, with crude tools and weapons they fashioned from stone.

As the glaciers continued to melt and the climate warmed, more plants and animals became available for food. People began to move throughout Canada. As people settled in different regions, they developed diverse characteristics and ways of living. Indians in the prairie region of central Canada were nomadic, which means that they traveled around from place to place. They searched for the best bison-hunting grounds and lived in tepees, conical tents made of animal skin stretched over a pole framework. Woodland Indians in the eastern forests lived in semipermanent villages and hunted deer and smaller game.

On Canada's west coast, Indians lived in permanent villages of solid wooden buildings and hunted whales and other sea life. In the arctic north, other descendants of Asian wanderers, the Inuit, lived in ice huts called igloos and hunted seals, whales, and caribou.

For thousands of years, Canada's Indians and Inuit lived in almost complete isolation from the rest of the world. Then European explorers discovered their lands.

The First Europeans

The first Europeans to set foot on Canadian soil apparently were Vikings, intrepid Scandinavian sea raiders and explorers. In about A.D. 1000, a Viking party under the leadership of Leif Eriksson sailed westward from Greenland. Some time later, they landed on the shores of North America, at a place Eriksson named Vinland.

Historians dispute the exact location of Vinland. Some believe it was in what is now Massachusetts or Maine in the United States, whereas others think it was in Canada. Archaeologists have unearthed a small Viking settlement on the island of Newfoundland, at a place called L'Anse aux Meadows, that some believe was the first settlement in Vinland.

After the Vikings, no other Europeans made contact with Canada for more than 400 years. In 1492, Italian explorer Christopher

Sebastian Cabot, like his father, John, was one of the skilled navigators who explored the coast of Canada in the 1500s. It is possible he sailed into Hudson Bay, mistaking it for the Pacific Ocean.

Columbus sailed westward across the Atlantic Ocean from Spain in search of a quicker route to the Indies, as Europeans of the time called Asia. But instead of reaching Asia, Columbus landed in the Caribbean islands of North America.

News of Columbus's voyage sparked others to cross the Atlantic in search of easy riches. In 1497, England's king Henry VII hired Italian navigator John Cabot (born Giovanni Caboto) to search for an even more direct western route to the Indies. Cabot reached shore somewhere between Newfoundland and Nova Scotia and claimed the land for England. The next expedition Cabot led was lost at sea, but in 1508 his son Sebastian sailed west and probably discovered Hudson Bay, which he supposed was the Pacific Ocean. Although neither

Cabot found the great riches they and King Henry VII had hoped for, John Cabot found waters so thick with fish that he reported trouble sailing his boat through them. Lured by the elder Cabot's reports, fishing fleets from England, France, and Portugal began to work the rich Grand Banks fishing grounds off the coast of eastern Canada, hauling in abundant harvests of cod and other valuable edible fish.

New France

By the early 1500s, Europeans realized that Columbus and Cabot had discovered a new continent. Many called this continent the New World. In 1534, Frenchman Jacques Cartier sailed from France to the New World to search for gold and other metals. Cartier sailed into the Gulf of St. Lawrence and landed on the Gaspé Peninsula in what is now New Brunswick, which he claimed in the name of King Francis I of France. On a second trip, in 1535, Cartier sailed up the St. Lawrence River to the site of present-day Montreal, where rapids prevented further ship travel. On a third visit in 1541, Cartier was part of a French expedition that attempted to establish a permanent settlement in Canada. This settlement lasted only until 1543.

Following Cartier's voyages, French fishermen came to Canada's waters in increasing numbers. These fishermen built whaling and fishing stations along the Atlantic coast and began to trade with the Indians. In return for knives, kettles, cloth, and other goods, they received beaver furs from the Indians. At the time, hats made from beaver skin were extremely popular throughout Europe.

Realizing the fortune to be made from the fur trade, the French made plans to establish a colony, to be called New France, in Canada. In 1604, under the direction of King Henry IV, French explorer Pierre du Gua established a small settlement—Île de Ste. Croix— near the mouth of the St. Croix River in what is now New Brunswick.

The following year, these settlers moved to the Annapolis Valley in Nova Scotia, then called Acadia, and founded the village of Port Royal.

Although this settlement endured for a time, it never really prospered. In 1613, an English expedition from the British colony of Virginia burned Port Royal and drove the French away. The French

A painting depicts French settlers being expelled from the colony of Acadia by the British in 1758. Many resettled in present-day Louisiana, where the word Acadian *turned into* Cajun. *There, they preserved their culture and language, and their descendants add to the French influence in the state today.*

returned and reconstructed their settlement, only to greet an expedition of 72 people from England who arrived to settle there in 1627. King James I of England had claimed the area as British and given it to a Scotsman, who named it Nova Scotia (New Scotland in Latin). The French and British coexisted uneasily in the area for years, until some of the French were expelled in 1755 and the remainder in 1758.

Far to the north, in 1610, another English expedition had made its way into Canada. The search for furs was not what drove this group but rather the search for another route to the Far East. Some explorers and navigators believed that a route to China and the Indies could be found by sailing northwest from Europe in search of a passage to the Pacific Ocean like the Strait of Magellan, discovered in 1520 at the tip of South America. Martin Frobisher, Henry Hudson, and John Davis were among those who sailed in search of this fabled Northwest Passage. In 1610, Henry Hudson discovered the enormous bay that bears his name in the far northeastern part of Canada, but his expedition ended in personal disaster when his starving crew mutinied and set him, his son, and seven others adrift in the bay in a small rowboat. Hudson's party perished, but one mutineer guided the ship back to England, and the English extended their presence in Canada.

In 1608, a French explorer named Samuel de Champlain established a settlement on the St. Lawrence River that he named Quebec. Under Champlain's guidance, the settlers made friends with the native Algonquin and Huron Indian tribes and began to trade with them. He also helped these tribes in their battles against the Mohawk and Iroquois tribes in what is now New York. In 1609, the French colonists and the Hurons defeated the powerful Iroquois in battle, in part because of the guns the French possessed. In one stunning show of force, Champlain aimed a gun at a group of four Iroquois chiefs. With one shotgun blast of four pellets, two chiefs fell dead, and the rest fled in terror. From that point on, the Iroquois were sworn enemies of the French.

The French enjoyed such good relations with the Hurons that Champlain wished to take one back to visit France. In exchange, he left one of his men, 18-year-old Étienne Brûle, to spend the winter with the tribe. When Champlain returned, Brûle dressed like a Huron, canoed like a Huron, and spoke the language fluently. The Huron who had been to France was appalled at conditions there and returned to his tribe, but Brûle remained and traveled with various Indian tribes for the next 20 years of his life, until his behavior

The French explorer Samuel de Champlain, who founded Quebec in 1608, did much to strengthen the French presence in Canada.

toward Huron women so enraged that tribe that they chopped him to pieces and made him the main course at a feast.

Champlain encouraged Roman Catholic missionaries, particularly an order known as the Jesuits, to introduce Christianity to the Hurons. The Jesuits quickly moved throughout the Canadian interior, exploring the area now known as southern Ontario and Quebec and founding the settlement of Montreal.

Despite Champlain's work, Quebec remained a small settlement, with only about 60 residents in 1625. Moreover, Montreal was under threat of Iroquois attack. The Iroquois had overrun the Huron lands and killed many French missionaries, traders, and settlers, nearly destroying the French fur trade.

Concerned about the future of New France, King Louis XIV made the colony a royal province of France. He sent an able administrator named Jean Talon to oversee its government and development, and he sent French troops to fight the Iroquois. Gradually, the troops convinced many Iroquois to make peace.

By the late 1660s, New France was once again open for trade and settlement. The fur trade flourished, and farmers began to clear and work land in the St. Lawrence River valley. New France's population grew rapidly during this period, increasing from about 3,000 in 1666 to 6,700 in 1673, and its boundaries expanded as well. Fueled by the thought of profits to be made in the fur trade, explorers roamed throughout the Great Lakes and the Ohio and Mississippi valleys. They claimed all lands they visited in the name of France. And wherever explorers went, traders—and eventually settlers—followed.

Traders and guides (known as *coureurs de bois* and voyageurs) ranged into the wild woods of the north in search of Indians with whom to trade. A young French trader, Médard Chouart des Groseilliers, was arrested and fined by the authorities of New France for fur trading without the permission of the governor. After his release, the disgruntled Groseilliers went to the British and told them of the great bounty of furs in the Hudson Bay region, hoping they would aid him in bypassing the French.

In 1670, Groseilliers and a party of traders sailed a small ship, the *Nonsuch*, into Hudson Bay and returned to England with a load of luxuriously rich beaver pelts. The furs made the backers of the party rich, and King Charles II granted a charter to the party, which included his nephew Prince Rupert, count palatine of the Rhine and duke of Bavaria. Rupert was one of Charles's favorite relatives because he had courageously defended the English monarchy, and the esteem in which Charles held him may help explain the generosity of the charter, which gave the group of investors, known as the

France and Britain both possessed colonies in North America and fought four wars between 1689 and 1763.

A N
A C C O U N T
OF THE
LATE ACTION
OF THE
New-Englanders,
Under the Command of
Sir *WILLIAM PHIPS*,
Against the
FRENCH
A T
CANADA.
Sent in a
Letter from Major *Thomas Savage* of *Boston* in *New-England*, (who was present at the Action) to his Brother Mr. *Perez Savage* in *London*.
Together with the Articles of War composed and agreed upon for that purpose.

Licensed April 13. 1691.

London, Printed for *Thomas Jones* at the *White Horse* without *Temple-Bar*, 1691.

Hudson's Bay Company, title to the entire Hudson Bay watershed (the area watered by the rivers that drain into Hudson Bay). The 1.5 million square miles (3,885,000 square kilometers) of territory was promptly named Rupert's Land.

The new trading company established a British outpost, the Hudson's Bay Colony, that quickly became a major threat to French trading interests and to the continued expansion of New France. To the south, the 13 burgeoning American colonies of England also checked New France's growth.

At this time, France and England were already enemies, having been at war for more than 100 years in Europe. In the colonies, religious differences—French Roman Catholicism versus British Protestantism—added to the tension.

Beginning in 1689 and ending in 1763, French and British colonists fought four wars. The final, decisive one was known as the Seven Years' War in Europe and as the French and Indian War in North America. The British, with superior numbers of troops and aided by the powerful Iroquois, captured Quebec City in 1759 and Montreal in 1760 and forced France to sign the Treaty of Paris in 1763. The treaty required France to surrender most of New France to England.

British Colonies

After defeating France in the Seven Years' War, England turned its attention to its new lands in Canada. First it changed the colony's name from New France to Quebec, then added some of the new territory to the colonies of Newfoundland and Nova Scotia. After a brief attempt to anglicize the French, the British—under the Quebec Act of 1774—eventually let the French settlers retain their language, their Roman Catholic religion, their laws and customs, and their farmland. Discontent was growing in the 13 colonies to the south,

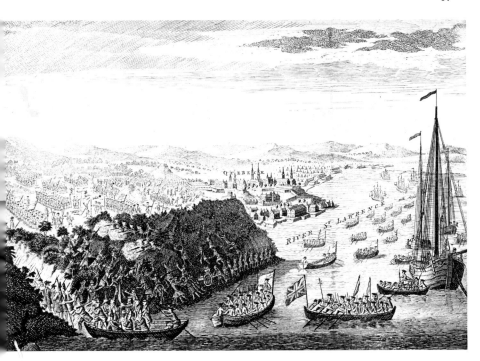

On September 13, 1759, forces under British general James Wolfe defeated those of French field marshal Louis Joseph de Montcalm on the Plains of Abraham and took the city of Quebec for England. Four years later, France signed away all claims to Canadian territory in the Treaty of Paris.

and the British hoped to make allies of the French in Canada in the event that the colonists revolted.

But those restless colonists also sought the support of the French Canadians in their planned rebellion. However, the French regarded both the British and the 13 colonies to the south with equal distrust, for both groups were English Protestants. In addition, land speculators from Virginia coveted the area of the Ohio and Mississippi rivers, where the French dominated the lucrative fur trade. The French took no clear-cut side in the American Revolution when it began in 1775. Early in the war, the Americans attempted to invade Canada but failed.

During the revolutionary war, many American colonists remained loyal to England. They were known as United Empire Loyalists, and about 40,000 of them moved to Canada (some during and others after the war) and settled mainly in Nova Scotia and Quebec. Other American-born settlers also moved north during this time to escape the fighting or join Loyalist relatives.

The rapidly increasing population changed the nature of the Canadian colonies. In the east, Britain created a new colony of New Brunswick out of the western part of Nova Scotia. In Quebec, the new British settlers quickly tired of living under the French laws and customs. They demanded a government based on the British system.

As a result of their protests, the British government in 1791 split Quebec into two large colonies, Upper Canada (the area around the Great Lakes and the upper St. Lawrence River) and Lower Canada (the area surrounding the lower St. Lawrence River). Each colony had its own elected assembly, although the assembly had little power. The colonies were governed by lieutenant governors and legislative assemblies appointed by the British Crown. Most of the people in Upper Canada were British. Here the colonial government followed the traditions of English law. In Lower Canada, the French were in the majority, and government was based on the French system.

Westward Exploration

The American Revolution changed not only Canada's political structure but also its economic structure. After the war, many of the prime fur-supplying areas in the Ohio and Mississippi valleys became part of the United States. In need of new sources of furs, the traders looked to other areas. In 1784, British merchants formed a company

(continued on p. 57)

SCENES OF
CANADA

▲ *The first settlers in the Maritime Provinces of Nova Scotia depended on both fishing and farming to support themselves. These canoes and rowboats are docked in Peggy's Cove, Nova Scotia.*

◄ *The Buchart Gardens in Victoria, British Columbia, protect and display several of the many species of flowers that thrive in Canada.*

∨ *On the Ross Farm in Nova Scotia, oxen draw a load of wood.*

▼ *These young hikers gaze out over Moraine Lake, in Banff National Park, Alberta, Canada's first national park.*

▲ *Wildflowers spring to life along a stream in Dinosaur Provincial Park in Alberta, one of the Prairie Provinces. The park is named for the enormous number of particularly well preserved dinosaur fossils discovered there.*

▲ *Canada has not only preserved its wilderness in its parks but has also made it easily accessible. These visitors stroll along the shores of Lake Louise, in Banff National Park.*

▼ *The Magdalene Islands, in the center of the Gulf of St. Lawrence in eastern Canada, have a coastal beauty all their own.*

⋏ *The old and the new meet in a reflection in a modern glass tower in downtown Toronto. Canada's urban landscape can be as striking as its vast wilderness.*

(continued from p. 48)

to conduct trade west and north of the Great Lakes. The North West Company sent explorers out into the unknown western region in search of new fur-trading areas.

Alexander Mackenzie, a partner in the North West Company, became obsessed with finding a waterway to the Pacific. After mistakenly following for 2,653 miles (4,245 kilometers) the river that now bears his name, he wound up on the shore of the Arctic Ocean instead. In 1793, he formed another party and tried again, following a different river. Mackenzie and his party succeeded in reaching the Pacific coast, becoming the first Europeans to traverse the breadth of Canada. Other explorers followed. Simon Fraser discovered and named the Fraser River in 1808, then followed its flow to the Pacific Ocean. David Thompson mapped the western lands and canoed the entire length of the Columbia River in 1811. Thompson was an excellent navigator and geographer and impressed even hostile Indians with his ability to know just where he was nearly all the time. His wife, Charlotte Small, accompanied him on his treks and helped paddle a canoe, sometimes even while pregnant with 1 of their 16 children. On the canoe trip down the Columbia River, she brought an infant and two toddlers with her.

Traders, then settlers, soon followed these intrepid explorers westward. One of the first and most important settlements was established in 1812 by a Scottish earl named Lord Selkirk, who led Scottish and Irish immigrants to the banks of the Red River (in what is now Manitoba). Slowly, his and other western settlements began to prosper.

In the same year, war broke out between Great Britain and the United States. During the War of 1812, U.S. troops twice tried to invade Canada but were turned back each time. Although the war ended in a stalemate in 1815, Canadians claimed victory and gained a new sense of patriotism and unity.

Voyageurs *transported canoes and supplies on their back for hundreds of miles deep in the wilderness for* coureurs de bois, *who trapped beavers for their valuable fur. Their search for wealth led them to explore much of the continent and helped drive Canadian expansion to the Pacific Ocean.*

The Pacific Coast

On the far western coast of the continent, exploration and settlement proceeded much more slowly. Spanish explorers were the first Europeans to reach Canada's Pacific coast, sailing up from their settlements during the 18th century in what is now California. By 1798, the Spanish had given up all claims to the area to the British. British and American traders visited the coast from time to time, but the region remained largely undeveloped. The navigators who reached the coast overland did so for the North West Company, which controlled the area until merging with the Hudson's Bay Company in 1821. The latter company retained control of the territory until 1869.

In addition, the U.S.-Canada border west of the Mississippi was not clearly defined. After the War of 1812, the diplomatic conventions of 1817 and 1818 set the boundary at the 49th parallel (one of the equally spaced east-west lines with which geographers and mapmakers encircle the globe) as far west as the Rockies, but the boundary was not extended to the coast until 1846. Until 1848, when gold was discovered in the Fraser River valley, the population west of the Rockies remained quite small, and traveling fur traders outnumbered settlers.

Bytown was a small settlement in Ontario when Queen Victoria declared it the capital of the British province of Canada. In 1867, when the Dominion of Canada was formed, Bytown was renamed Ottawa and became the capital of the Dominion.

Making a Nation

Canada's population soared in the early 1800s, fueled mainly by thousands of immigrants from Great Britain. As the population grew, so did political unrest. Both Upper and Lower Canada felt that they were not represented fairly in their legislative assemblies and that the Crown exerted too much influence over their affairs. In addition, as English speakers flocked to Canada, including both Loyalists after the American Revolution and British immigrants, tensions grew as the proportion of French speakers dropped.

In 1837, a fiery French-Canadian leader named Louis-Joseph Papineau proposed that Lower Canada unite with the United States. He had not always been so radical, but his experience as Speaker of the Lower Canadian Assembly and the way in which the British Parliament had ignored a petition signed by 87,000 French Canadians had made him despair of achieving more freedom by legal means. In October 1837, Papineau led a small rebellion that the British monarchy quickly and brutally suppressed. However, Papineau was one of the first political leaders to give French Canadians hope of gaining power and a degree of autonomy.

Inspired by Papineau's rebellion and by the example of American democracy, a small group of Upper Canadian settlers under the leadership of Scottish-born radical William Lyon Mackenzie revolted against the pro-British government of Upper Canada. This rebellion, too, ended in ignominious defeat.

Although both rebellions failed, they did lead to the Crown's investigation of the conditions behind them. Worried that the colonies had serious internal problems, 19-year-old Queen Victoria sent British diplomat Lord Durham to look into the situation in 1838. A liberal politician nicknamed Radical Jack for his sympathy for democracy, Lord Durham was an able adviser. His report, completed in 1839, recommended that Upper and Lower Canada be united and that the Canadian colonists be given more say in their own affairs.

In 1840, the British Parliament passed the Act of Union, which united the two colonies into one, known as the Province of Canada, composed of Canada West (formerly Upper Canada) and Canada East (formerly Lower Canada). However, although this act changed the political structure of Canada, it actually did little to loosen British control.

Throughout the 1840s, several colonial leaders continued the struggle for increased independence from Britain. In 1848, the Province of Canada and the colony of Nova Scotia finally achieved such independence through a system of self-government known as *responsible government*. In this system, the government leader is responsible to (that is, must answer to) an elected legislative assembly. Gradually, Britain granted responsible government to almost all regions of Canada.

But despite the new freedom and power provided by responsible government, the Province of Canada remained troubled by political divisions. French-speaking and English-speaking colonists vied for local control. The main opposition political parties had nearly equal representation, so no party could stay in power more than a few months at a time. This situation greatly slowed the province's economic and social development. Frustrated by the constant turmoil, political leaders started to campaign for a *confederation* (union) of all the British North American provinces and colonies. Many of these leaders were backed by wealthy railroad owners and bankers, who

The Fathers of Canadian Confederation *by Robert Harris depicts the leaders who met at an 1864 conference in Quebec to discuss confederation. The resolutions passed there formed the groundwork for the British North America Act.*

thought national unity would pave the way for westward expansion. Others, wary of the growing power of the United States to the south, pushed for unity for reasons of security.

In 1867, the British Parliament passed the British North America Act, uniting the Province of Canada and the Atlantic colonies of Nova Scotia and New Brunswick into the Dominion of Canada. The Province of Canada (composed of Canada East and Canada West) became the provinces of Quebec and Ontario. Not all the provinces were in favor of confederation. In particular, many colonists in Nova Scotia and New Brunswick strongly opposed it, and the provinces of Newfoundland and Prince Edward Island were not included in the confederation, although provisions were included in the act allowing them, as well as the Hudson's Bay Colony territory and the British colony of British Columbia on the Pacific coast, to join at a later date.

The British North America Act granted the Dominion only limited powers of self-government. It specified a governmental system based on the British parliamentary system, with a British governor-general presiding over an appointed Senate and an elected House of Commons. The leader of the party with the most members in Parliament became the prime minister. The queen of England remained monarch of Canada, and Great Britain retained control of the relationship between the Dominion (still technically a colony) and foreign powers. Sir John A. Macdonald, the leader of the majority Conservative party, was appointed the Dominion's first prime minister in 1867. Except for a five-year period from 1873 to 1878, he remained the Dominion's prime minister until he died in 1891.

The Railroads and Expansion

The new Dominion grew quickly in the late 1800s. One of Prime Minister Macdonald's major goals was to expand the Dominion to the west. The Oregon Treaty of 1846 had extended the U.S.-Canada border along the 49th parallel to the Pacific coast. When gold was discovered in the Cariboo Mountains in the west, thousands of fortune seekers flocked to the area, many from California. To prevent the United States from attempting to claim the rapidly growing area, Great Britain had formed the colony of British Columbia in 1858; this colony did not become part of the Dominion of Canada under the British North America Act. In 1869, the Canadian government purchased claims to the western lands from the Hudson's Bay Company, and Great Britain agreed to hold its northwest colonies for Canada until they could be absorbed into the Dominion.

However, westward expansion did not go smoothly. A large group of western colonists based around the Red River in Rupert's Land disputed the Dominion's claim to the lands. Many of the settlers were *métis*—persons of mixed French-Canadian (therefore Roman Catholic) and Indian ancestry. They feared that the arrival of many British Protestant settlers would threaten their lands and their very way of life. Métis spokesman Louis Riel headed a provisional government elected by the Red River settlers and led a rebellion from 1869 to 1870. He hoped to negotiate acceptable terms for entry into the Dominion. But in 1870, Riel authorized the execution of Thomas

Scott, an anti-Catholic agitator who had plotted to assassinate Riel. The execution sparked a clash between the new settlers and the métis. British and Canadian troops quickly helped the settlers overcome the métis, and Riel, who had become a hero to French-speaking Canadians, fled.

The Dominion took possession of Rupert's Land. It also acquired the vast Northwest Territory from Great Britain. Later in 1870, the government created Canada's fifth province, Manitoba, from part of Rupert's Land. The northern remainder of Rupert's Land was joined with the Northwest Territory, and the whole area was called the Northwest Territories.

The Pacific coast colony of British Columbia became the Dominion's sixth province in 1871, in exchange for the government's promise to construct a railway linking the Atlantic and Pacific coasts. In 1873, the colony of Prince Edward Island also joined the Dominion as the seventh province.

By the late 1870s, Canada's provinces stretched from ocean to ocean, but travel and communication between eastern and western provinces was difficult. At this time, the fastest way to get from Montreal to British Columbia was through the United States, on its transcontinental railway. A railway stretching from coast to coast through Canadian territory was needed to unite the emerging nation.

From its proposal in 1871, the massive Canadian Pacific Railway construction project was plagued by scandal and mismanagement. Prime Minister Macdonald and his Conservative government fell from power for five years, charged with corruption over the awarding of railroad contracts. Actual construction did not even begin until 1878.

The work of building a transcontinental railroad was a formidable task. The builders had to blast through mountains of granite to carve tunnels and railbeds from the rugged western terrain. Engineers had to design and erect miles of bridges over rivers and

A newspaper illustration depicts armed supporters of Louis Riel, métis settlers who resisted incorporation into the Dominion in 1869–70 in the Red River area and in 1884–85 in Saskatchewan. Riel led both rebellions; both failed.

marshes. Many thousands of workers were needed, and the need was met by unskilled Chinese and Irish immigrants. Although the work was very dangerous, the construction companies gave little regard to worker safety. In the worst section, it was estimated that one Chinese worker died for every railroad tie laid.

Finally, on November 7, 1885, at Craigellachie, British Columbia, Canadian Pacific Railway official Lord Strathcona drove the final spike in a ceremony celebrating the completion of the railroad. Shortly afterward, the first transcontinental train steamed from Montreal to Vancouver.

The transcontinental railroad opened up both the midwestern and western provinces for trade and settlement. The métis, who had moved westward into Saskatchewan after their failed rebellion in 1869, once again found their land in jeopardy. From 1884 to 1885, Louis Riel led another métis uprising, known as the Saskatchewan Rebellion. More than 7,000 government troops rode the new railroad west and quickly crushed the revolt. Riel was found guilty of treason and executed, causing outrage among French speakers. His death permanently alienated the Province of Quebec from the ruling Conservative party, sowing more seeds of separatism.

Throughout the rest of the 19th century, settlers streamed into the Canadian prairie region. The development of new strains of wheat, well suited to Canada's harsh climate, meant that farmers could make huge profits growing and selling grain. Hundreds of thousands of immigrants from Europe and thousands more from America took up farming on the prairies. By 1905 the best agricultural lands in Canada had been settled, and wheat had become the Dominion's chief export crop. That year, the government divided the prairies into two provinces, Saskatchewan and Alberta.

During this period, Canada's cities also grew rapidly. Most of the 2 million immigrants who came to Canada between 1896 and 1911 settled in eastern cities, such as Montreal and Toronto.

In the vast north, mining spurred exploration and development. Construction of the Canadian Pacific Railway in 1883 uncovered the world's largest nickel deposit at Sudbury in north Ontario. Discovery of petroleum and other minerals in the north followed government mapping and surveying expeditions.

On April 16, 1896, George Carmack and two Indians struck gold on a stream that flowed into the Klondike River in the far northwestern Yukon region of Canada. The ensuing gold rush brought hordes of prospectors, miners, and other fortune seekers to the area. Driven by "Klondicitis," or "gold fever," these eager adventurers flocked to the region in a movement known as the "Klondike stampede." The new town of Dawson sprang up almost overnight at the junction of the Yukon and Klondike rivers, near the rich goldfields. But most of the new arrivals were disappointed because the best claims had already been staked by the time they arrived. Of the estimated 100,000 who set out for the Yukon, only about 20,000 actually panned for gold; of these, only 4,000 found any. Most of the new arrivals ended up selling their possessions to raise enough money to travel home.

Those lucky few who struck it rich became known as the "Klondike Kings." Most spent their newfound riches carelessly in the gaudy saloons and dance halls that lined Dawson's Front Street. For

At the height of the Klondike gold rush, some miners paid for their supplies with gold dust just panned from the river.

several brief years, Dawson flourished; some called it the "San Francisco of the North." Though gamblers, swindlers, and assorted lowlifes thronged the city, little of the open violence and robbery that marked boom towns in the western United States was to be seen. But after the excitement died down, most of the new arrivals moved on. Today, Dawson is a quiet town of about 1,500 people, most of whom work for the government or in the tourist industry.

The Indian Question

Continued expansion of Canadian settlements and trading had dire consequences for Canada's native Indian tribes. When Europeans first landed on the Atlantic coast, an estimated 200,000 Indians lived in Canada.

Except for scattered outbreaks of violence, for several hundred years Indians and the new settlers coexisted in relative harmony. But as the settlers' demands for land increased, the Indians fell on hard times. Settlements spread through their hunting grounds and drove out the bison and other animals on which the Indians depended for food. Traders supplied warring tribes with guns and cheap rum, which encouraged violence and alcoholism. These factors, along with the Indians' susceptibility to new diseases (introduced by the white settlers and to which they had no immunity), devastated the Indian population. Only about 100,000 Indians remained in Canada by 1900. Concerned by the Indians' plight, the Canadian government began to establish *reserves*, lands set aside for Indian settlement.

Toward Independence

Canada flourished in the early 20th century. Its farmers produced enormous wheat harvests—what the Canadians did not consume was sold to European nations for handsome profits. Mineral exports also brought much wealth to Canada. The steel and textile industries grew rapidly, and new railroads helped open up more lands for farming, mining, and logging.

Streams of immigrants who arrived too late to get good prairie land poured into Canada's cities at the turn of the century. The narrow streets of Quebec City may have reminded some of their European homeland.

Canadians contributed greatly to Great Britain's effort in World War I. Canada sent infantrymen, airplane pilots, and cavalry— more than 600,000 soldiers in all.

But as Canada's wealth grew, so did a new spirit of dissatisfaction with British rule. For Canada still remained subject to British policies regarding foreign affairs, including matters of trade and, most particularly, of war and peace.

When Great Britain entered World War I against Germany in 1914, tens of thousands of Canadian men volunteered for military service. Canadian soldiers first saw action in April 1915 and served valiantly throughout the war. Canada also contributed to victory from the sky. Its most famous combat pilot, Billy Bishop, shot down 72 German planes during the war. More than 600,000 Canadians served in World War I, and more than 63,000 died.

Canada's industrial capacity increased greatly as the wartime demand for ships, artillery shells, and other equipment helped the steel industry expand. War-ravaged Europe needed food, and Canada increased its agricultural production, especially of wheat and beef.

This economic growth, combined with the fine service record of the Canadian armed forces, produced a new confidence among the Canadian people. They began to feel they were a nation separate from Britain, with a very different character and economic status.

During the war, the issue of *conscription* (the draft, or forced military service) caused a rift between Canada and Great Britain. When war first broke out, large numbers of Canadian volunteers rendered a draft needless. However, as the war ground on and casualties mounted, the number of Canadian volunteers dropped sharply, so Prime Minister Robert Borden, leader of the Conservative party, began the draft in July 1917. Most English-speaking Canadians supported the policy, but French Canadians bitterly opposed it. Despite their opposition, Borden went ahead.

As a result, Borden's Conservative party lost power in Parliament, and he was forced to reorganize his political support. But he remained prime minister and became increasingly dissatisfied with Canada's status as a mere colony of Great Britain—especially in light of Canada's important contributions to the Allied effort in World War I. After the war ended, he demanded, and received, more say in developing the British Empire's policies on defense and foreign affairs. In 1919, Borden forced Great Britain to allow Canada to sign the Treaty of Versailles (the formal end of the war) on its own behalf. Canada also applied for separate membership in the brand-new League of Nations, an organization of world nations formed in 1920 as an international peacekeeping body.

In 1922, William Lyon Mackenzie King, leader of the Liberal party, succeeded Borden as prime minister. King was even more determined than Borden to establish Canada as an independent nation—and even more willing to clash with the Crown. First, he refused to pledge Canadian troops to aid Britain in a threatened war with Turkey. Then, in 1923, he signed a fishing treaty with the United States. It was the first time Canada had acted independently from Britain in an agreement with a foreign power.

Prime Minister King traveled to London in 1926 to attend an imperial conference with representatives of the British government and all British dominions (or former colonies). At this conference, the dominions won recognition as equal members of the British Commonwealth of Nations, as the British Empire then became known.

Finally, on December 11, 1931, the British Parliament enacted the Statute of Westminster, which recognized Canada and some other British Commonwealth dominions as independent nations.

A Young Nation

The newly independent Canada got off to a somewhat rocky start. In 1929, the collapse of the New York Stock Exchange triggered the Great Depression in the United States, and its effects soon reached Canada and the rest of the world. Thousands of Canadian factories, mines, and stores and other businesses closed down. Hundreds of thousands of Canadian people lost their jobs; many thousands also lost their homes. The price of wheat dropped sharply at the same time that a severe, prolonged drought in the Prairie Provinces devastated the wheat crop and worsened the situation.

Canada's increasing prosperity and strength during the 1920s attracted these unemployed British miners to the prairies as farm workers.

The depression lasted until the outbreak of World War II. Canada declared war on Germany in September 1939, following the lead of Great Britain and other European nations. It declared war on Japan on December 8, 1941, the day after the Japanese surprise attack on the U.S. Navy base at Pearl Harbor, Hawaii.

Canadian forces fought all over the world during the war. By the war's end in 1945, more than 1 million Canadian men and women had served in the armed forces. Nearly 100,000 lost their life in the fighting.

The war helped restore Canada's depression-ravaged industrial economy, as factories and steel mills increased production to meet the Allied demand for machinery and supplies. During the war, the Canadian government also started several important social programs. Some of them have endured to the present day, including social security, unemployment compensation, financial aid to families with young children, and veterans' benefits.

The Canadian economy continued to thrive after the war ended. The discovery of oil and gas in Alberta in 1947 and the development of iron mining helped spark a construction boom that fueled Canada's rapid change from a basically agricultural nation to one of the world's leading industrial powers. Another wave of immigration between 1946 and 1955 brought more than a million people from war-torn Europe, most of whom settled in Toronto, Montreal, and other cities, leading to rapid urban and suburban growth. The opening of the St. Lawrence Seaway, an impressive engineering accomplishment, in 1959 allowed huge oceangoing ships to reach the Great Lakes.

Canada's ever-increasing economic strength and prestige made many Canadians more interested in their nation's role in international affairs. In 1945, Canada became an original member of the United Nations (UN). In 1949, it entered into a defense agreement with the United States and 10 Western European nations known as

Icebreakers carried U.S. and Canadian officials through the St. Lawrence Seaway at its formal opening on April 25, 1959. A joint U.S.-Canadian effort, the seaway took five years to build.

the North Atlantic Treaty Organization (NATO). Canadian forces served in the Korean War between 1950 and 1953 as part of a UN force dispatched to resist North Korean expansion into South Korea.

In the 1950s, Canada and the United States cooperated in building an early warning radar system across Canada. The two nations signed the North American Air Command Defense (NORAD) agreement in 1957, integrating the air defenses of Canada and the United States.

A Nation Matures

The 1960s brought new problems for Canada. The economy sagged, and unemployment rose sharply. In Quebec, many French Canadians began to demand the separation of Quebec from the rest of Canada. They wanted to establish Quebec as an independent French-speaking nation.

Out of this political turmoil, the Liberal party rose to power. In 1963, Liberal leader Lester B. Pearson became prime minister. Pearson quickly set about developing new social service programs, including a national pension plan in 1964 and a national health insurance program in 1965. He also persuaded the Canadian Parliament to adopt a new national flag. First flown on February 15, 1965, the new flag featured a red maple leaf on a white field between two red bars. All symbols of the historic ties with Britain had been removed.

In 1967, Canada celebrated the 100th anniversary of its confederation with a world's fair called Expo 67. Held in Montreal, this popular fair drew visitors from around the world.

Prime Minister Pearson resigned in 1968. His successor, Pierre Trudeau, was Canada's third French-Canadian prime minister and one of its most popular prime ministers ever. Trudeau discouraged the French-Canadian separatist movement and instead tried to bring English- and French-speaking peoples together under one national banner by passing laws designed to promote equal opportunity and equal treatment for all Canadians. But although his policies brought some major changes to Canadian government and society, they had little effect on the growing separatist movement.

The 1970s saw new hopes for economic expansion in Canada. It also saw new strains developing in the relationship between Canada and the United States over issues such as U.S. ownership of Canadian companies and the effects of U.S. industrial pollution on Canada's environment.

The Quebec separatist movement grew in strength during the 1970s. A group called the Front de Liberation du Quebec (FLQ) began using terrorist tactics, including kidnapping and murder, to call attention to their plans for separation. The government eventually crushed the FLQ, but the separatist movement continued. A

French-Canadian separatist sentiment grew throughout the 1960s. These marchers protested the celebration of British queen Victoria's birthday as a national holiday.

separatist political party called the Parti Quebecois gained control of Quebec's provincial legislature in 1976. Under the leadership of René Lévesque, Quebec's new prime minister, the province held a special vote on a proposal designed to lead to independence for Quebec. Despite all the talk about separation, however, Quebec's voters rejected this proposal by a six to four margin.

Controversy about Quebec's status continued through the 1980s and 1990s. The Meech Lake agreement, signed in 1987, would have provided constitutional protection to Quebec's distinct language and culture, but this accord broke down by 1990. Then a new wave of separatist sentiment led to a 1992 national referendum on a proposal to give Canada's most populous regions (including Quebec) greater representation in Parliament. The proposal was defeated. In 1995 Quebec itself held another referendum on its future, and the proponents of secession lost by only a small margin.

The activism of French-speaking Canadians helped raise the militancy of other ethnic groups as well, including native peoples such as the Inuit (Eskimos), the Cree, and the Iroquois. Nevertheless, the 1980s and 1990s saw some progress in the nation's relations with its multitude of ethnic groups. In 1988 the Multiculturalism Act officially established Canada as a land of diverse cultures. In 1992, in the Northwest Territories, voters approved the creation of a self-governing homeland for the Inuit.

This broad issue of unity in diversity may be the dominant one for years to come. Despite Canada's rank as one of the world's major economic powers, its great wealth of natural resources, and its excellent quality of life, many Canadians believe the key to their country's future will be its ability to knit its many distinct groups into a unified whole.

One of the most popular and controversial Canadian prime ministers in history, the charismatic Pierre Elliott Trudeau led the government from 1968 to 1979 and from 1980 to 1984. A prime minister appoints a cabinet and is leader of the majority party in parliament.

Canadian Government

Canada's system of government shows the influence of both the United States and Great Britain. It combines a central, or federal, government, patterned after that of the United States, with a cabinet system, and includes the individual governments of each of the nation's 10 provinces and 2 territories. Although each of the provincial and territorial governments has some power of self-government, all must answer to the central government in Ottawa.

Canada's cabinet also includes the central government's legislative and executive branches. The legislative branch, known as Parliament, is made up of two houses, the Senate and the House of Commons. Members of the Senate are appointed by the governor-general and the prime minister; members of the House of Commons are elected by popular vote. All Canadian citizens over the age of 18 are eligible to vote.

The structure of the government is partly based on the written constitution of Canada and partly on unwritten, customary ways of doing things. For example, the cabinet system is not described in the constitution but is always part of government. The written part is based on the Constitution Act of 1982, which includes the British North America Act, the document that spelled out the Canadian government's role from 1867 to 1982.

One of the major purposes of the Constitution Act of 1982 was to end once and for all the influence of Great Britain on Canadian government affairs. Before the act, the British Parliament had to approve all amendments to Canada's constitution. Now amendment approval is based solely on the decisions of Canadian provinces. If any 7 provinces with a total of more than 50 percent of the nation's population approve an amendment, it becomes law.

The Constitution Act of 1982 included other provisions as well. A Charter of Rights gives Canada's Supreme Court the power to determine whether laws passed by Parliament violate the constitution. If a law is found to violate the constitution, the Supreme Court can cancel it.

The constitution stipulates the division of power between Canada's federal government and its provincial and territorial governments. The federal government is responsible for matters affecting the entire nation, such as federal taxation and other monetary policies, national defense, and foreign relations. Provincial and territorial governments are responsible for most local matters, such as education, justice, and civil law.

The Crown

Even though the Constitution Act of 1982 formally ended Great Britain's influence on Canadian law, Queen Elizabeth II of Great Britain remains queen of Canada and the official head of state. She holds only a symbolic role, however, and has no real power in Canadian government. The prime minister actually directs the government.

The queen's representative in Canada is known as the governor-general. At one time, the governor-general always came from Great Britain, but since 1952 all of them have been Canadian. The Canadian prime minister actually chooses the governor-general but the queen makes the ceremonial appointment.

A governor-general usually serves from five to seven years, performing only certain formal and symbolic tasks, such as giving the address at the opening of each session of Parliament. Over the past several decades, the office has alternated between English-speaking and French-speaking appointees. In 1984, Jeanne Sauvé became Canada's first female governor-general.

The Prime Minister and the Cabinet

The prime minister is the actual head of Canadian government. Curiously, however, the constitution does not even mention the prime minister's role. The office evolved out of a similar position in Great

Prince Charles visits with children at a boys and girls club during an official visit to Canada. Although there has been no change in the Canadian government's official position in recognizing the British monarch as the formal head of state, many Canadians favor a change in this policy.

Britain's government. By tradition, the prime minister is an elected member of Parliament (M.P.) and the leader of the House of Commons's majority party (the political party with the most members in the House of Commons). Under the direction of the majority party, the governor-general appoints the prime minister.

The prime minister holds office only as long as the majority party grants its support. If a prime minister loses the majority party's backing, he or she must either resign or ask the governor-general to call a new general election in an attempt to regain support.

By granting or withholding support, Parliament influences the actions of the prime minister. As long as the majority party can obtain a majority of votes in the House of Commons, it can pass the bills it wishes, and the prime minister remains in power. But if the majority party loses the majority of votes, it has to depend on the support of opposition-party members to remain in power. If the House of Commons defeats a major item sponsored by the majority party, such as a new budget, the prime minister resigns, and a general election is held. But the prime minister in turn can control Parliament by asking the governor-general to dissolve the House of Commons and call for a new general election at any time.

The cabinet helps the prime minister run the government. It consists of 30 or so members, or ministers, chosen by the prime minister from the House of Commons's majority party and sometimes from the Senate. Each cabinet minister usually heads a government department. The duties of cabinet ministers are varied. Government ministries such as agriculture, communications, environment, finance, fisheries and oceans, justice, labor, defense, health and welfare, transportation, and veterans' affairs deal with government functions that affect nearly every Canadian. Other ministries deal with the functions necessary to run the government itself.

Because cabinet ministers are elected officials, they may lose their positions if they lose their seats in Parliament. For this reason, each government department has a deputy minister—a civil servant (government employee)—who serves as the department's permanent administrative head.

The Senate

The Senate, the upper house of Parliament, consists of 104 members. They are not elected by a vote of the people but rather are appointed by Canada's governor-general under the direction of the prime minister. Members serve until they reach age 75, at which time they must retire. The Senate's presiding officer, known as the Speaker, is also appointed by the governor-general based on the prime minister's recommendation. Usually, each new prime minister recommends the appointment of a new Speaker.

The Senate's membership is distributed regionally, not strictly according to population. The Atlantic Provinces—Newfoundland, Prince Edward Island, Nova Scotia, and New Brunswick—have a total of 30 members in the Senate. The most populous provinces, Quebec and Ontario, each have 24 members. The western provinces of Alberta, British Columbia, Manitoba, and Saskatchewan send a total of 24 members. The Northwest Territories and the Yukon Territory each have one member. This regional distribution ensures that all areas of Canada are represented in the Senate.

Even though the Senate is the upper house of Parliament, it has less power than the lower house, the House of Commons. The senators cannot introduce or reject bills involving taxes or issues involving the spending of money. They can introduce other types of bills and can propose amendments to bills passed by the House of Commons, which must still be approved by the House of Commons before they become law. One of the Senate's most important functions is to debate issues and prepare reports for presentation to the House of Commons.

Recently, some Canadians have proposed changes in the Senate. They are concerned that the prime minister appoints members

The Senate and House of Commons meet in the Houses of Parliament, which overlook the Ottawa River and dominate the city's government center.

mainly as rewards for political favors, such as raising campaign funds. But changing the Senate would require modification of Canada's constitution, something that would probably take many years to accomplish.

The House of Commons

Although officially the lower house of Parliament, the House of Commons actually has far more power than the upper house, the Senate. Most of the important bills, including all those involving taxes and government spending, originate in the House of Commons.

The House of Commons has a total of 301 members of Parliament, or M.P.s. Each M.P. represents a *constituency* (voting district) of a Canadian province and is elected by popular vote in that constituency. (An M.P. does not have to live in the constituency, or even the province, that he or she represents.) The number of M.P.s from each province is based on the population of that province and changes with each Canadian census count. Each M.P. serves a term of five years unless an election is called earlier. If that happens, as is often the case in Canadian politics, the M.P. must run for reelection.

Like the Senate, the House of Commons has a speaker who presides over its meetings. Unlike the Speaker of the Senate, who is appointed by the prime minister, the Speaker of the House is elected by a vote among the M.P.s. The Speaker serves until the next general election.

Provincial and Territorial Governments

Each of Canada's 10 provinces and 2 territories has its own government. Canada's governor-general appoints a lieutenant governor for each province. Like the governor-general, the lieutenant governors hold largely honorary positions. In nine provinces, a premier actually heads the government. In Quebec, this function is performed by an official known as the prime minister.

The provincial governments are organized much like the federal government except that provincial legislatures have only one house instead of two. In nine provinces, this house is called the Legislative

Assembly; in Quebec, it is known as the National Assembly. Although provincial governments control most internal matters, the federal government has the power to reject any law passed by a provincial legislature. However, it rarely uses this power and has only rejected about a hundred out of the many thousands of laws passed by the provincial legislatures.

The two territorial governments have traditionally held less power than the provincial governments, but that arrangement has

The Royal Canadian Mounted Police, established as the Northwest Mounted Police in 1873, have a long and honorable history. They enforce federal legislation throughout Canada and provincial legislation in all provinces except for Quebec and Ontario and are the only police force in the Yukon and Northwest Territories.

been changing in recent years. The Yukon Territory has an elected head official known as the government leader and an elected legislative assembly of 17 members. In the Northwest Territories the government is led by a premier, and the legislative assembly has 24 members headed by a speaker.

Local Government

Local government is regulated by provincial and territorial governments. Each province is divided into counties, or districts, which in turn are further divided into cities, towns, villages, and townships. Each of these municipalities is governed by an elected council. Elected heads of these local councils are usually called mayors, reeves, wardens, or overseers. Elected council members are known as councillors, aldermen, or controllers. Local councils provide such services as road maintenance, garbage pickup, water supply, and police and fire protection. The provincial governments provide funds, mostly from property taxes, to the local governments.

Judicial System

Canada's judicial system includes the Supreme Court, the Federal Court, and the provincial courts. Judges are appointed by the governor-general based on recommendations of the prime minister. The Supreme Court, Canada's highest court, is composed of the chief justice of Canada and eight associates, called puisne judges. The Supreme Court hears appeals from Federal and provincial courts.

The Federal Court includes two divisions, a trials division and an appeals division. The trials division, which consists of an associate chief justice and seven puisne judges, tries all claims affecting the federal government. The appeals division, which has a chief justice and three puisne judges, mainly considers appeals from the trials division. Provincial courts administer both federal and provincial laws.

Armed Forces

In 1940, Canada and the United States formed the Permanent Joint Board of Defence to cooperate in the defense of both nations. In 1968, Canada's army, navy, and air force were merged into one entity called the Canadian Armed Forces (CF). Any Canadian citizen be-

Although Canada remained officially neutral in the Vietnam War, a number of Canadians fought in the conflict. In 1986, at the first reunion of Canadian Vietnam veterans in Washington, D.C., a mother is shown to her son's name engraved on the Vietnam Veterans' Memorial.

tween ages 19 and 24 who has completed eighth grade may enlist in the CF for 5 years.

The CF is under the command of the chief of the defense staff, who reports to the minister of national defense, a member of the prime minister's cabinet. The CF includes five commands: the Air Command, the Maritime Command, the Land Forces Command, the Communications Command, and the Training Command. Formerly the CF Europe Command, stationed in Germany, provided Canada's contingent of troops for the North Atlantic Treaty Organization (NATO). In 1992, however, with the Cold War ending, Canada decided to withdraw its combat troops from NATO command.

Canada's wilderness provides more than opportunities for recreation. Canada is a modern, highly industrialized nation, and its natural resources—including a variety of minerals, extensive reserves of oil and natural gas, and cheap hydroelectric power—are essential to its economy.

Canadian Economy

Canada is one of the world's most prosperous nations. Its gross domestic product (GDP) — the total value of all goods and services it produces — ranks in the top 12 of the world. More than 98 percent of the GDP comes from service businesses such as insurance and banking and from industry. Agriculture accounts for about two percent.

Private enterprise forms the basis of the Canadian economy, meaning that individuals and corporations own and run most businesses. But in recent years the federal and provincial governments have become increasingly involved in economic activities. The government now owns utilities, broadcasting companies, transportation services, and steel and petroleum (oil) companies. It also has become involved in the housing industry and in the management of natural resources. In addition, the federal government provides health insurance to guarantee medical care for all Canadians.

The strength of Canada's economy depends in large part on its trade with other nations. The United States is Canada's most important trading partner, accounting for over three-quarters of all exports and imports. Other major trading partners include Japan, the United Kingdom, and Germany. In recent years Canada has actively sought to expand its trade with the Asia-Pacific region, especially the rapidly growing nations of the Pacific rim.

A significant issue for many Canadians is the apparent dominance of their economy (and therefore some parts of their culture) by the United States. Recent events have reinforced this concern. In the late 1980s the Canadian government committed itself to trade liberalization — that is, the lifting of trade barriers such as tariffs. Then in 1994 the North American Free Trade Agreement (NAFTA) went into effect, providing for the eventual elimination of all tariffs between Canada, the United States, and Mexico. Though these changes have brought new opportunities for Canadian business and have stimulated the rise of high-tech industries, they have also prompted increased alliances between Canadian and U.S. firms. Many Canadians have expressed renewed worry that their economic fate is not in their own hands.

More than 70 percent of all Canadians work in service businesses. These Toronto bank and financial workers staged a road race in suits and ties and called it the Rat Race to illustrate an old cliché about business.

The Canadian economy has been transformed during the 20th century. At the turn of the century, more than half of all employed Canadians earned their living on farms, in mines, or in forests. Today, Canada is a modern industrialized nation whose people work in many different fields. More than 73 percent of Canadians are employed in service businesses, and about 15 percent work in manufacturing industries. Less than seven percent work in agriculture, mining, forestry, and fishing.

Service Sector

The service sector includes a wide range of occupations, primarily in community, business, and personal services. The most important businesses in this sector include banks, insurance companies, and other financial institutions; hospitals; schools; restaurants and other food-service businesses; import-export services; transportation services; and communications companies.

These last two areas, transportation and communications, are especially vital for a nation that covers such a huge geographic expanse. Canada's rapid economic growth in fields like computer software and telecommunications bodes well for the future.

Manufacturing

Canada's second-most important economic sector is manufacturing, which can be divided into two major categories: export industries, which produce goods for trade with other nations, and domestic industries, which manufacture goods for use by Canadians. Each category accounts for about half of Canada's industrial output.

Most of Canada's industries are concentrated in its major cities, especially the cities of Quebec and Ontario provinces. In fact, factories in Quebec and Ontario produce more than three-fourths of all manufactured goods in Canada. The major industries include food processing, paper and paper products, and transportation equipment.

Canada's food-processing industry mainly prepares meat and poultry. Other important products include bread and other grain products, dairy products, canned and frozen vegetables and fruits, soft drinks, beer and ale, and whiskey.

Canada is the world's largest exporter of wood and paper products and the leading producer of newsprint, on which newspapers are printed. It produces over one-quarter of the world's newsprint. The paper industry is centered in Quebec, with factories located throughout the eastern forests.

In Canada, transportation manufacturing focuses on automobiles and automobile parts. Every major U.S. automaker operates factories in Canada; most are located in Ontario, across the Great Lakes from Detroit. Canadian auto plants produce more than 1.3 million cars each year. Other transportation equipment manufactured in Canada includes trucks, farm machinery, and airplanes.

Other important Canadian industries include chemicals, electronic equipment and metal machinery manufacturing, steel production, and oil refining. Traditionally Canada's manufacturing industries were concentrated in the east. Recently, however, western cities like Vancouver, Calgary, and Edmonton have gained an increasing share.

Canada's manufacturing industries require huge amounts of electricity to power their operations. Most of the electricity is generated by hydroelectric power plants located on large rivers in Quebec, Ontario, British Columbia, and throughout most of the other provinces. For example, a large hydroelectric plant on the St. Lawrence River at Niagara Falls provides electricity for southern Ontario. Because hydroelectric plants generate electricity from the force of running water, they are extremely clean sources of energy. Nuclear power plants and coal-burning plants are other important sources of electricity.

Oil, natural gas, and coal are Canada's other major energy sources. Canada produces about 700 million barrels of oil each year.

About 82 percent of it comes from the Province of Alberta. Canada also imports oil from foreign countries, primarily for use in the eastern provinces. Natural gas, a plentiful and relatively clean fuel, provides about 28 percent of Canada's energy needs. Most of Canada's natural gas comes from Alberta and British Columbia. Coal supplies less than 15 percent of the energy used in Canada. Most Canadian coal is mined in Alberta, Saskatchewan, and British Columbia.

The Canadian government is constantly searching for new sources of energy. Possible future energy sources may include hydroelectricity generated by the tides in the Bay of Fundy, solar energy, windmill-generated electricity, and wood- and peat-burning power plants.

Forest Industries

About half of Canada's land area is covered by forests, and forest products are the nation's single largest export. The United States is the major customer for Canada's forest products, consuming more

Nearly 100 feet higher than Niagara Falls, Montmorency Falls tumbles over a cliff near Quebec City. Eastern Canada, poor in oil and gas, relies on the area's many rivers and waterfalls to produce clean, cheap hydroelectric power.

than 60 percent of Canada's total exports. The leading timber-producing provinces are British Columbia, Ontario, and Quebec.

The federal and provincial governments own about 90 percent of Canadian forestland and lease the land to private companies for logging. Loggers cut down and transport Douglas fir, hemlock, spruce, pine, and other evergreens as well as assorted hardwood varieties. Sawmills in western and eastern Canada process the trees into lumber and useful wood products, including wood chips and sawdust. Pulp and paper mills, located mainly in the Canadian Shield area and on the Atlantic coast, process trees into wood pulp and paper.

Today, much of Canada's forestland faces the threat of acid rain, a serious form of air pollution. Acid rain results from the release of sulfur dioxide and nitrogen oxide into the atmosphere from coal-burning industries and power plants, many of them in the industrial centers of the United States. Westerly winds carry the emissions to the forests of eastern Canada, where they damage trees and kill plant and animal life in lakes and rivers. Acid rain is one of the major sources of dispute between Canada and the United States. Many Canadians believe that the U.S. government is not doing anything to stop industries and utilities from releasing harmful emissions into the atmosphere.

Agriculture

Canada has approximately 169 million acres of farmland. Major agricultural products include wheat, oats, barley, livestock, and dairy products. Canada is one of the world's largest producers and exporters of wheat. More than half of the wheat it exports is grown in the Province of Saskatchewan, with most of the rest coming from Manitoba and Alberta. Most of Canada's beef cattle are raised on ranches in Alberta. The Prairie Provinces, which encompass more than three-fourths of Canada's farmland, also produce vegetables, alfalfa, sugar beets, hogs, poultry, and other agricultural products.

Canada's other major agricultural area is the St. Lawrence low-lands in southern Quebec and Ontario. Important products in this area include beef cattle, other livestock, milk and cheese, fruits, vegetables, and tobacco.

Although the western provinces are not considered important agricultural areas, dairy farms, cattle ranches, fruit orchards, and chicken farms dot the region. The Okanogan Valley in British Columbia is Canada's leading apple-growing center.

The Canadian government has established marketing agencies to help protect farmers from wide fluctuations in the demand for and the price of agricultural products. The government also provides farmers with technical and business-management assistance. Despite government help, however, the number of farms and farmers is steadily declining for several reasons. Farms are becoming larger and more highly mechanized, which means that fewer farmers are

Wilcox, Saskatchewan, is one of the small rural communities that dot the Prairie Provinces' enormous stretches of farmland. Fewer and fewer Canadians choose to live in such isolated areas, but Canada remains a leader in agricultural production.

needed to work them. And each year many thousands of acres of prime farmland are being lost to development—especially in the populous areas of southern Ontario and Quebec. Although agricultural production is more than adequate for today's population, some Canadians are worried about the future consequences of the continuing loss of farmland.

Mining

Canada is the world's leading exporter of minerals and the leading producer of uranium, potash, and zinc. It is the second-leading producer of asbesto, nickel, sulphur, and cadmium. Other important minerals include copper, aluminum, platinum, lead, and gypsum. However, oil, natural gas, and coal provide more than half of Canada's mineral income. The mining industry has helped open up remote regions of Canada for settlement and has been an important factor in the nation's economic growth. Although relatively few people work in the industry itself, mining plays a vital role in many other sectors of the Canadian economy. For example, factories employ Canadians to make mining machinery, and import-export firms process mineral transactions.

Canada's mineral storehouse is the name sometimes given to the Canadian Shield region in northeastern Canada, where most mines are in remote, isolated areas. Often, only a single railroad line links a small mining settlement with the outside world. These settlements depend solely on the mines for their survival, and if the mines shut down, the town usually dies.

Fishing

Fishing is one of Canada's oldest industries. As far back as the 1500s, European crews fished the waters off the Atlantic coast and brought their catches back to Europe. Even today, the Grand Banks off the

Abundant schools of herring and cod support a substantial Canadian fishing industry.

coast of Newfoundland is one of the world's richest fishing grounds. Although the industry has declined severely in recent decades, fishing is still a significant source of income for the Atlantic Provinces and some areas of British Columbia.

In the Atlantic, important fish and shellfish include cod, herring, lobster, and scallops. Salmon is the major product of Canada's Pacific fisheries, with the prime fishing areas located in the mouths of the Fraser and Skeena rivers in British Columbia. Other important Pacific species include halibut and herring. On both coasts, processing factories located on the waterfront freeze and can the catches directly from the fishing boats. Besides ocean fishing, Canada also has some of the world's best freshwater fishing areas. Principal commercial species, which are sold mainly in central Canada and the United States, include pickerel, perch, pike, whitefish, and smelt.

Many fishers are concerned with the steady decline of Canada's fishing industry. They point to overfishing by foreign fleets as the main cause of the decline, and they are urging the Canadian government to limit foreign access to the waters off Canada's coast.

The Inuit were the original residents of northwestern Canada but now are only a tiny proportion of the population. Like other elements in the Canadian mosaic of peoples and cultures, they are part of modern Canada but hold on to their heritage.

Canadian Faces, Canadian Lives

By 1997, Canada's estimated population surpassed 30 million people, more than double what it was in 1951. A high birthrate and steady immigration account for the rapid increase. About 4 million people immigrated to Canada from 1951 to 1977 alone. They came from all over the world, but mostly from Great Britain, Germany, Greece, Italy, and other European countries. Political refugees from places such as Eastern Europe and Southeast Asia have also found new homes in Canada. Still, the majority of Canadians are of British or French descent.

Many Canadians of British ancestry, especially those in the Maritime Provinces, are descendants of Scottish settlers who began arriving in the 1700s; others descend from British and Irish immigrants who arrived in the 1800s. Some are descendants of the United Empire Loyalists, who migrated north to Canada during or after the American revolutionary war.

French-speaking Canadians are concentrated in the Province of Quebec, the only province where they are in the majority, although other provinces, including Ontario, New Brunswick, and Nova Scotia, have significant French-speaking populations.

Canadians of German descent, numbering about 1.5 million, live mainly in Ontario, the Prairie Provinces, and Nova Scotia. Most Italians, the next-largest group, have settled in the big cities, particularly Toronto and Montreal. Canada also has about 500,000 citizens of Ukrainian descent, the majority of whom live in the Prairie Provinces.

The west coast has a large number of residents of Asian descent. Chinese, Japanese, and other Asians make up over three percent of the population of Canada as a whole. Immigrants from China and the Caribbean islands have recently established thriving communities in Toronto.

Indians and Inuit, Canada's native peoples, now account for less than two percent of the population. The name *Eskimo* comes from an Indian word meaning eater of raw meat. The Eskimos, however, call themselves *Inuit*, which in their language means people. Most of Canada's 30,000 Inuit live in the remote arctic north in the Yukon Territory and Northwest Territories. A 1992 vote provided that an

Canada's growing Asian community includes these young Chinese immigrants in Toronto.

Inuit homeland called Nunavut ("Our Land") would be carved out of the Northwest Territories by 1999.

Today about 375,000 Indians of various tribes live in Canada, mostly on more than 2,000 reserves. Major tribes include Algonquin, Athapaskan, Haida, Iroquois, Kootenai, Salish, Sioux, Tlingit, Tsimshian, and Wakasha.

On the reserves, Indians have long struggled to maintain some semblance of their native culture while also adapting to modern Canadian life. For a long time it seemed that they were losing this struggle, as poverty, unemployment, alcoholism, disease, and hopelessness ravaged the reserves. Today, however, there is a new spirit alive among Canada's Indians. Their native culture has proved too deep and strong to be destroyed and is now a source of pride and strength. Indian arts—including paintings, carvings, prints, and beadwork—are prized by collectors the world over. A new type of Indian leader is starting to examine and, when necessary, to challenge the legality of old treaties and agreements. The Indians are demanding a louder voice in running their own affairs, and the Canadian government may be starting to listen.

Canada is a bilingual nation, meaning that is has two official languages. Throughout the land, road signs and other messages appear in both English and French. Canada's bilingualism reflects its history as both a British and a French colony. Today, even though English-speaking and French-speaking residents are equally Canadians, the differences nurtured through more than 400 years of Canadian history have made each group unique.

Because Canada is a vast, varied country, its people have many different ways of life. Many of the dissimilarities result from cultural background or regional location. For example, a French-Canadian family living in an apartment in Montreal certainly spends the day differently from a farm family descended from German immigrants on the prairies of Saskatchewan, an Inuit family in a remote Yukon settlement, or a Japanese family in Vancouver. But within the general classifications of urban life, rural life, and arctic-wilderness life, distinct patterns of living emerge.

Urban Living

Today, 77 percent of Canadians live in urban areas, where life is similar to that in the cities of any other modern industrialized nation. Many people live in crowded high-rise apartment buildings and ride buses or subways to work in high-rise office buildings. Others who live on the city's outskirts commute by car on expressways. Rush hour brings traffic jams just like those occurring in cities all over the world.

Three out of four Canadians are city dwellers. This apartment complex, called Habitat, was built in Montreal for Expo 67 to demonstrate new models for urban living.

City dwellers can choose from a wide variety of cultural attractions and recreational activities, including concerts, plays, movies, museums, parks, and athletic events. Dining out and going to a show is a popular nighttime activity. On most nights, however, the source of entertainment is that old standby, the television set. Weekends are a time for relaxation. By law, most stores and businesses must remain closed on Sunday, so few people work on this day.

Although Canadian cities are large and modern, they generally do not have as many severe social problems as the large cities in most other countries. Crime rates, for example, are still relatively low, though they have climbed enough in the past decade to alarm many Canadians. To a visitor from the United States, most Canadian cities seem remarkably clean, prosperous, and well run. But beneath the surface, some signs of trouble are beginning to appear. Recent government reductions in funding for housing, transportation, education, and health care may lead to future problems. New racial and ethnic tensions are sprouting as immigrants pour into the cities.

Rural Life

About 23 percent of Canadians live in rural areas — 6 percent of them on farms. An increasing number of country dwellers commute to a city each day for work. Others work in village businesses or in such industries as mining, fishing, and logging.

Most Canadian farmers own their farms. Because modern farm machinery allows farmers to do nearly all their farm work themselves without outside help, farms have become larger and larger, but farming remains primarily a family affair. Family farms are commonly passed down from generation to generation. Canada's largest farms are located in the Prairie Provinces, where farms average 850 acres (344 hectares) in size. In contrast, farms in central and eastern Canada average only about 240 acres (97 hectares).

In rural areas, villages and small market towns are the centers of social activity. Here, families shop, go to church and school, seek medical care, find entertainment, and participate in community activities.

Wilderness Life

Very few people live in the vast arctic wilderness of the Yukon and Northwest Territories. Indians and Inuit, the region's native residents, today make up about 50 percent of the region's population. Other residents of the arctic wilderness include oil- and gas-industry workers, miners, traders, and members of the CF and the Royal Canadian Mounted Police.

Progress is slowly making its way to the Arctic. As a result, the Inuit and Indians face a dilemma. Some continue to follow the traditional ways and their traditional occupations of hunting, trapping, and fishing. But the benefits of modern life are attractive, and almost all the Inuit and Indians now live in modern houses, wear modern clothes, eat modern foods, and drive snowmobiles and motorboats in place of dog sleds and kayaks.

Holidays and Celebrations

Canadians celebrate several national holidays. The most important is Canada Day, July 1. Once known as Dominion Day, this holiday is Canada's official birthday, marking the creation of the Dominion of Canada by the British North America Act in July 1867. The celebration includes patriotic ceremonies, picnics, and fireworks displays, much like the Fourth of July in the United States.

May 24th is Victoria Day, celebrated to commemorate the birthday of Queen Victoria of Great Britain. In Quebec, where residents have no wish to celebrate the birthday of a British queen, this holiday is called Dollard Day, commemorating Dollard des Ormeaux, a 17th-century French soldier who gave his life valiantly defending Montreal against Iroquois raiders. To Canadians, this holiday marks the beginning of summer. Labour Day, celebrated on the first Monday in September, as in the United States, marks the end of the summer season and the beginning of the new school year.

Other holidays are also similar to those celebrated in the United States, although sometimes with slight variations. Canadians celebrate Thanksgiving with a traditional roast turkey and all the fixings but do so on the second Monday in October instead of the last Thursday in November, as in the United States. Christmas Day, New Year's Day, and Easter are on the same dates as in the United States.

Sports and Recreation

Canadians love the outdoors and take advantage of the many recreational opportunities their beautiful land offers. In wintertime, popular outdoor activities include skiing, ice-skating, snowshoeing,

For many, the preeminent Canadian sport is ice hockey. Young players idolize great skaters and players, and legions of fans follow the fortunes of the Canadian National Team. Here, the goalie for Japan (right) blocks a Canadian's shot at a world ice hockey meet.

tobogganing, snowmobiling, and ice fishing. Warm-weather pastimes include swimming, fishing, boating, cycling, camping, hunting, hiking, tennis, and golf.

Canada's extensive national park system provides ideal areas for many of these activities. The first Canadian national park, Banff National Park in Alberta, was established in 1885. The park system now includes 37 national parks and more than 700 national historic parks and sites. Each province and territory has at least one national park in addition to its own provincial and territorial parks.

Millions of Canadians enjoy amateur and professional sports. By far the most popular sport is ice hockey. Canada's first national amateur hockey league was organized in the 1880s. Today, the National Hockey League (NHL) includes 26 teams from major cities in Canada and the United States. Each year, millions of fans attend games and/or watch them on television. Star players are revered as national heroes. Hockey is even more popular on the amateur level. Starting at age seven, children can compete in organized leagues in most communities throughout Canada. The Canadian National Team, made up of star amateur and professional players, represents Canada in Olympic and other international competitions. And outside organized teams and leagues, groups of players can be found engaged in spirited pickup games on almost every patch of ice big enough to hold them.

Canadians also love baseball and football. Both popular games are U.S. imports. In baseball's major leagues, the Montreal Expos and Toronto Blue Jays compete with U.S. teams, and the Blue Jays in 1992 became the first team based ouside the United States to win a World Series. In professional football, the Canadian Football League (CFL) has fielded teams representing cities all across Canada, and its championship game is one of the most-watched sports events in the nation.

More traditional Canadian sports, still widely played and watched, include lacrosse and curling. Lacrosse was Canada's first national game, played by Indians before the first Europeans arrived. Curling, a traditional Scottish sport, was adopted by Canadians long ago. In this unique game, players propel large round stones along an ice surface toward a target while other players use brooms to sweep the ice in front of the sliding stone to help it travel farther and more accurately.

Quebec's Cirque du Soleil troupe is an inventive, experimental group of performers who have toured the United States to wide acclaim.

Arts and Entertainment

Canadians value art and entertainment highly. Encouraged by the government, which in 1957 set up the Canada Council to promote artistic advancement, the arts have flourished in the 20th century. The council provides financial assistance to individual artists and to groups such as orchestras and dance and theater companies. In addition, most provinces support the arts. The federal government also sponsors several arts centers for the presentation of theater, dance, and music productions. One such facility is the National Arts Centre in Ottawa, opened in 1969. The government-sponsored National Gallery, also in Ottawa, displays a large and important collection of works by artists from Canada and throughout the world.

Canadian artists produce a wide range of work reflecting the enormous cultural diversity within Canada. Until the mid-1800s, Canadian artists generally followed European traditions. Then new Canadian artists started to develop their own distinct style and to emphasize Canadian subjects. Cornelius Krieghoff, born in the Netherlands but working in Quebec, painted realistic scenes of French-Canadian farm life. Canadian-born Paul Kane used the Indians of western Canada as his subjects.

Not until the beginning of the 20th century did the first truly distinctive Canadian style of painting develop. A group of landscape painters known as the Group of Seven broke from the traditional realistic style to paint highly individualized, brightly colored scenes of the Canadian wilderness. The Group of Seven opened the doors for other distinctive artists in the 20th century, including Emily Carr, David Milne, Jean-Paul Riopelle, Harold Town, Alexander Colville, and Jean-Paul Lemieux.

Native Canadian arts and crafts are prized by collectors worldwide. Inuit and Indian sculptors fashion beautiful carvings from ivory, stone, and wood. Some painters and printmakers incorporate

Margaret Atwood's thought-provoking novels include Cat's Eye, Surfacing, Bodily Harm, *and* The Handmaid's Tale. The Handmaid's Tale *was a best-seller and was made into a movie.*

traditional geometric patterns; others use modern techniques. Their works depict native legends and myths as well as the wildlife of the north country. The native Canadian artistic heritage is fostered by such contemporary artists as Norval Morrisseau and Daphne Odjig, who have exhibited their work throughout the world.

Canadian writers, like artists, also produce a diverse body of work. Literature in Canada has a long and rich history. It can be divided into two basic branches: French-language works and

English-language works. Although these two branches grow out of different literary traditions, both reflect the history and experience of Canada. The most characteristic titles share a common thread of "Canadianism" that emphasizes such factors as nature and Canada's place in the world. The many Canadian writers known the world over include novelists Robertson Davies, Margaret Atwood, Mordecai Richler, and Michael Ondaatje and poets E. J. Pratt, A. M. Klein, Earle Birney, and Irving Layton.

Theater flourishes throughout Canada, and regional theater organizations are based in most provinces. Well-known theatrical events include the Stratford Festival, held each year in Stratford, Ontario; the Shaw Festival in Ontario; and the Festival Lennoxville in Quebec. Le Théâtre du Nouveau Monde in Montreal is the leading theatrical organization in French-speaking Canada.

Canadians have made important contributions to the world of music. In classical music, the late, brilliant pianist Glenn Gould is still revered for his interpretations, and singers like Jon Vickers, Louis and Gino Quilico, and Maureen Forrester have gained worldwide fame. In popular music, well-known Canadian performers include Neil Young, Joni Mitchell, Bryan Adams, Shania Twain, k.d. lang, Alanis Morissette, and Céline Dion.

Canada also has several outstanding symphony orchestras, including the Montreal Symphony Orchestra, the National Arts Centre Orchestra, the Toronto Symphony Orchestra, and the Vancouver Symphony Orchestra. The Canadian Opera Company, based in Toronto, performs six major operas each year. Canada also has three large professional ballet companies — the Royal Winnipeg Ballet, the National Ballet of Canada, based in Toronto, and Les Grands Ballets Canadiens in Montreal.

The Canadian motion picture industry has gained worldwide recognition. The industry began with the founding of the National

Film Board in 1939. This government-sponsored organization has produced hundreds of award-winning documentaries, animated features, and other films. After New York and Los Angeles, Toronto has become the third-leading production center in North America for film and television programs, and Vancouver has risen to fourth place.

Education

Each province and territory operates its own public school system. Most of these systems consist of 12 grades; however, Quebec and Newfoundland have only 11 grades, and Ontario has 13. Education is provided free for all public school students. The literacy rate (percentage of Canadians over the age of 10 who can read) is 99 percent.

In some provinces, the school systems include parochial schools for students of different religious affiliations. For instance, Quebec's system provides separate schools for Roman Catholic and Protestant students. Classes are taught in French in the Roman Catholic schools and in English in the Protestant schools.

In most school systems, students must attend school from age 6 to 16. Students who graduate from public school may choose to go on to a university. Major Canadian universities include McGill University, the University of Toronto, the University of Montreal, Laval University, and the University of Ottawa. Canada also has many two- and three-year community, or junior, colleges. In Quebec, institutions called *collèges d'enseignement général et professionel* (colleges of general and professional instruction) offer a two-year course that high school graduates must complete before entering a Quebec university.

Along with its school system, Canada also has an extensive public library system. The National Library of Canada in Ottawa was established in 1953.

Religion

The largest religious group in Canada is Roman Catholic. About 14 million Canadians, mostly French speaking, belong to the Roman Catholic church. Protestants are the next largest religious group. Important Protestant denominations, or groups, include United Church of Canada, Anglican Church of Canada, Presbyterian, Lutheran, and Baptist. Other major religions represented in Canada include Judaism, Islam, Buddhism, and Hinduism.

Health Care and Social Services

The federal and provincial governments provide comprehensive health care and other social services to Canadians from birth until death. All provinces participate in the national health insurance program, which pays for doctors' fees and hospital costs. Because of good medical care, Canadians as a whole are a healthy people. Men have a life expectancy of 76 years; women, of 83 years. These are among the highest life-expectancy figures in the world, and they exceed U.S. life expectancies by three or four years. (Life expectancy is the number of years a baby born today can expect to live.) The infant mortality rate (how many infants die before the age of 1) is only 6 per 1,000 births, one of the lowest rates in the world. Canada has achieved these results while spending less than 10 percent of its gross domestic product on health care.

Unemployment insurance and workers' compensation programs protect those who lose their job or who are injured at work. Social security benefits and pensions from the Canada Pension Plan or the Quebec Pension Plan help ease the financial burdens of old age.

Communications and Transportation

Because Canada is so large, it particularly needs good communications and transportation systems. Canadians have responded to this need by building one of the most advanced communications networks in the world. Orbiting communications satellites tie together all of Canada and link it with the rest of the world. Canada has close to 20 million telephones, and the TransCanada Telephone System operates the world's longest microwave telephone relay system, which extends 3,980 miles (6,368 kilometers) across southern Can-

This mural depicting peoples of the world decorated the United Nations pavilion at the World Exposition in Vancouver in 1986. The theme of the exposition was communications and transportation—particularly appropriate for Canada, whose size makes both services essential.

ada. This system handles not only phone calls but also transmissions of television, radio, and computer data from coast to coast.

The Canadian Broadcasting Corporation (CBC) broadcasts television and radio programs in both English and French. CBC broadcasts reach 98 percent of Canadian households. Recently the Canada Television and Cable Production Fund was created to increase the production of high-quality Canadian programs.

Canada produces over 1,400 magazines and journals covering all areas of interest, including politics, sports, travel, fashion, and the arts. There are more than 100 daily newspapers in English or French, and the total circulation is about 200 papers for every 1,000 people. That is, on an average day, one out of five people purchases a newspaper, almost the same proportion as in the United States. Leading English-language papers include the *Star* and the *Globe and Mail* in Toronto, the *Journal* in Edmonton, and the *Sun* in Vancouver. Among the major French-language papers are *Le Journal de Montréal* and *La Presse* in Montreal and *Le Soleil* in Quebec City.

Transportation is as important as communications in linking the regions of Canada together. Canadians have built an impressive system of highway, railroad, water, and air transportation. Canada has more than 550,000 miles (880,000 kilometers) of roadways. The Trans-Canada Highway traverses central Canada, extending some 5,000 miles (8,000 kilometers) between St. Johns, Newfoundland, and Victoria, British Columbia.

About 44,000 miles (71,000 kilometers) of track enable Canada's railroads to transport people and goods throughout the nation. Canada's railroad system is the third largest in the world—only those of the United States and Russia are more extensive.

Along the St. Lawrence River and Seaway and the Great Lakes lie some of the world's busiest inland ports. Huge oceangoing ships sail into and out of the Great Lakes laden with import and export goods. Coastal seaports are also important trade centers, especially Vancouver, British Columbia, on the Pacific coast, and Halifax, Nova Scotia, and St. Johns, Newfoundland, on the Atlantic coast.

Canada has two large airlines to provide domestic and international air transportation, Air Canada and Canadian Airlines International. Smaller regional airlines and dozens of foreign airlines also service Canada. The busiest airports are Toronto International, Vancouver International, and Montreal International.

Wild deer still roam northern Alberta, one of the Prairie Provinces. Each province features an assortment of landscapes— Canada as a whole has an astonishing variety. Knitting together these disparate elements and building a truly national identity is possibly the greatest challenge Canadians face.

Into the Twenty-first Century

As a new century opens, Canadians must address many issues. Perhaps the most important is their effort to develop a genuine national identity, an authentic sense of national unity, and an understanding of what being Canadian really means.

This lack of national identity has deep historical roots. For most of its history, Canada was not a nation but a group of loosely allied provinces ruled by Great Britain, which had little interest in fostering a sense of unity among the colonists. Each province developed its own government, economy, and culture and competed with the other provinces for superiority. As a result, many Canadian people came to identify most strongly with their province, not with their nation.

Confederation in 1867 under the British North America Act and even final independence from Great Britain in 1982 under the Constitution Act did little to change this situation. Many Canadians still refer to themselves as Newfoundlanders, Quebecois, or Albertans first and Canadians second. The rivalry among provinces and regions remains surprisingly strong. For example, the discovery of abundant oil supplies in the western provinces, particularly Alberta, boosted the economy of these provinces at the expense of the eastern provinces, which had to pay high prices for heating oil. These prices were set by the provincial governments in the west. In the 1980s, however, after oil was discovered under the floor of the Atlantic Ocean off the coast of Newfoundland, the eastern provinces struck back. The federal government felt that because the oil was discovered offshore it belonged to the entire nation. Newfoundlanders disagreed, demanding the opportunity to exploit their own "oil boom" to boost their local economy.

Another factor hindering national unity is Canada's wide diversity of ethnic and cultural groups. The dissatisfaction of many French-Canadians, or Quebecois, is well known. Not only are Quebec separatists a major force within the province, but from 1993 through the 1997 election they were the leading national opposition party.

More so than other countries—the United States is a prime example—Canada encourages its people to retain their unique cultural and ethnic identities. If the United States has been called a melting pot in which ingredients blend together, Canada can better be described as a mosaic in which distinct, separate pieces compose a large picture. Besides the Quebecois, English, Scottish, Irish, Italians, and Germans, other important Canadian ethnic groups include Jews, Orientals, Ukrainians, Scandinavians, and of course the native Indians and Inuit. The federal government has even adopted a policy of multiculturalism (recognition of different cultures) to encourage Canadians to celebrate their ethnic roots. The Multiculturalism Directorate of the Department of the Secretary of State puts this policy into action through national, provincial, and local education and arts programs. As a result of this policy, many Canadians identify themselves not only by their province or region but also by their ethnic background. But although this attitude is welcomed by the government, it also means that ethnic identity often competes with national identity in the hearts and minds of many Canadians.

Another hindrance to national identity—and perhaps the most difficult to overcome—concerns Canada's relationship with the United States. More than 3 out of 4 Canadians live within 200 miles (320 kilometers) of the U.S. border. Because of this closeness, among other reasons, the United States continues to have an enormous impact on Canadian life.

Prime Minister Jean Chrétien speaks at a meeting of the General Assembly to commemorate the fiftieth anniversary of the United Nations. As Canada has grown, it has taken an increased responsibility in international affairs and continues to struggle against appearing overly influenced by the policies of the United States.

Economically, Canada remains dependent on the United States. It is still primarily an exporter of raw materials and an importer of finished goods, and the primary buyer of its exports is the United States. American investors continue to control a large percentage of Canadian industry.

Culturally, the U.S. influence may be even more pronounced. The most popular magazines in Canada—*Time*, *Newsweek*, and *People*—are published in the United States. Despite the fine programming offered by the CBC, when Canadians watch television, more often than not they tune in to shows originating from the United States. Pop music, fast food, fashion—all show the extent of U.S. influence.

In recent years, the Canadian government has taken steps aimed at decreasing such U.S. influence. Strong government support for the arts and entertainment has brought new recognition to Canadian artists, who no longer feel they must leave the country to achieve worldwide recognition. As just one example of Canada's emerging cultural industries, the exports of Canadian books increased 151 percent in a five-year period in the 1990s.

Despite these steps, however, national identity remains Canada's most persistent issue. How this issue is resolved will go a long way in determining the face and soul of Canada in the 21st century.

‹GLOSSARY›

British Crown The British monarchy.

Colony A territory located apart from its parent nation but governed by that nation.

Confederation The formal union of four Canadian provinces into the Dominion of Canada, enacted in 1867.

Coureur de bois French for "woods runner," or trapper.

Inuit What Eskimos call themselves, meaning "people."

Iroquois A group of Indian tribes that live in what is now northern and central New York. They were particularly powerful in the 16th and 17th centuries.

Jesuits An order of Roman Catholic missionaries that traveled throughout Canada beginning in the mid-1500s, introducing Christianity to the Indians.

Métis Canadians of mixed French-Canadian and Indian ancestry.

North Atlantic Treaty Organization (NATO) An association of 15 nations, including Canada, the United States, and 10 European nations formed in 1947 to promote mutual aid and common defense.

Parliament Canada's legislative body, consisting of the Senate and the House of Commons.

Permafrost The permanently frozen subsoil that lies under the tundra.

Prairie   A large area of level or gently rolling land naturally covered with lush grasses and few trees; forms a large part of Canada's midwest.

Province   An administrative district of Canada, somewhat analogous to a state in the United States; Canada has 10 provinces.

Quebecois   French-speaking residents of Quebec, Canada's center of French culture.

Separatism   A movement that proposes to make Quebec a separate nation independent from Canada.

Tundra   Terrain found in arctic regions, consisting of a spongy, waterlogged layer of soil over permafrost; treeless but supports mosses, lichens, and hardy flowering herbs.

Vikings   Seafaring Norsemen who reached the coast of Newfoundland in the 10th century.

Voyageurs   Men who transported furs and traders throughout western Canada in the 17th and 18th centuries.

◄INDEX►

PICTURE CREDITS

AP/Wide World Photos: pp. 81, 107; Janet Bennett/Taurus Photos: pp. 50, 51; T. W. Bennett/Taurus Photos: p. 54; The Bettmann Archive: pp. 14, 20, 27, 45, 60, 69, 72, 84, 95; Culver Pictures: pp. 36, 39, 41, 43, 47, 58, 63, 66; Eric Kroll/Taurus Photos: p. 102; Terry McKoy/Taurus Photos: p. 55; Richard Perrine/Taurus Photos: p. 52; Richard Quataert/Taurus Photos: p. 56; Reuters/Bettmann Newsphotos: pp. 16, 18, 25, 33, 88, 92, 100, 109, 111, 115; L. T. T. Rhodes/Taurus Photos: p. 49; Donna Sinisgalli: pp. 6–7; Frank Siteman/Taurus Photos: p. 104; Norman R. Thompson/Taurus Photos: p. 53; Russell A. Thompson/Taurus Photos: p. 31; UN/DPI Photo: p. 121; United Nations: p. 2; United Nations/Canadian Government: pp. 22, 97, 99; UPI/Bettmann Newsphotos: pp. 68, 70, 74, 76, 78, 86; J. Whitaker/Taurus Photos: pp. 90, 118